# PRACTICAL WESTERN TRAINING

# PRACTICAL WESTERN TRAINING

*Second Edition, Revised and Enlarged*

## By Dave Jones

*Foreword by Randy Steffen*

UNIVERSITY OF OKLAHOMA PRESS : NORMAN AND LONDON

By DAVE JONES

*Practical Western Training* (New York, 1968)
*How to Correct the Problem Horse* (Houston, 1972)
*The Western Horse: Advice and Training* (Norman, 1974)
*The Dave Jones Book of Western Horsemanship* (Houston, 1976)
*The Western Trainer* (New York, 1976)
*The Book of Bad Habits* (Houston, 1979)
*Making and Repairing Western Saddles* (New York, 1982)
*Practical Western Training*, second edition, revised and enlarged (Norman, 1985)

Library of Congress Cataloging-in-Publication Data

Jones, Dave, 1927—
   Practical western training.

   Includes index.
   1. Western riding. 2. Horses—Training. I. Title.
SF309.3.J66   1985      636.1'0886      85-40476
ISBN 0-8061-1949-7 (alk. paper)

The paper in this book meets the guidelines for permanence and durability of the Committee on Production Guidelines for Book Longevity of the Council on Library Resources, Inc. ∞

## TO MY TEACHERS

A horse trainer isn't born with the ability to train horses. He has his teachers who mold and shape him into what he eventually becomes.

## HARRY FOLTZ JONES

my father, had horses, as his father and grandfather had before him. Harry taught me the fundamentals and usually had some kind of horse around for me to fool with.

*Early in my career* I met

## JACK OLDHAM LINK

Jack showed me that I had a lot to learn and then did his best to show me how to go about learning it. I never met a human being with a more horse-related ability than Jack Link. He just didn't know what to do with it.

*A few years later* I landed a job working for

## CHARLES GEORGE ARAUJO

Charley had an instinct about which horses were the best. When I worked for him, he bought Poco Tivio. He later leased Doc Bar and took him to California. I learned a lot from Charley about reining, roping, and the reined stock horse. He taught me a lot about people as well as horses.

*Still later* I met

## ARTHUR KONYOT

when he was trainer-teacher for Arthur Godfrey. We were poker-playing buddies. Mr. Godfrey once told me that he thought Konyot was the best trainer in the world. Konyot made me think about different ways of doing things, and I incorporated methods I learned from him in my training.

*Last, but certainly not least,* I want to honor my wife,

## MARY P. ("MAC") JONES

At present she's caring for 16 stray dogs and me. Though she gets on my case a lot, no one has been more supportive when I needed it. Thanks, Mac.

# Foreword to the First Edition

## By RANDY STEFFEN

MANY books have been written about training horses. Unfortunately, not all the people who have written books about training horses are qualified to train horses, much less write about training, or for that matter, anything else. But I suppose the same can be said for every subject about which books are written.

Books are the keys that unlock the treasure chests of knowledge. Books written by people who are not qualified are deadly weapons, for they plant false information in the minds of those who thirst for knowledge and are starved for the infinite details that make knowledge useful and rewarding.

Skill in working with horses can never be attained just by reading. A man who desires to acquire the skill, and the pleasure such skill affords, must put into practice the things that good books on horse training tell him. But first he must have confidence that the book or books he has selected have been written by horsemen whose knowledge is sound and the result of long experience based on methods known to have withstood the test of time. Horse training is one of man's oldest skills, and as with all skills, there are correct ways to apply it—and there are ways that are less than correct.

Any book that attempts to tell its readers how to accomplish some specific task is most difficult to write in a style that remains free of boring repetition and an air of superiority. But here you will find a book that will surprise and delight you! Not only will you learn exactly how to go about training a western horse to do many things, but you'll find yourself relishing every word of it. Dave Jones's ability as a horse-man is equaled by his ability to tell you how to train a horse and entertain you through every sentence of it.

It's been my pleasure to know Dave for a long time, and I've followed his career from one end of the cow country to the other. I take my hat off to him as a master horse-man—one of the most serious I've ever known—and as a master at telling others how to train horses without being boring for a single moment. And you'll take *your* hat off to him when you see your horse responding to the things you'll learn in the pages of this book.

# Contents

|  |  |  | Page |
|---|---|---|---|
| Foreword to the First Edition, by Randy Steffen | | | vii |
| Preface | | | xi |
| Chapter | 1 | What to Look for in a Horse | 3 |
| | 2 | Developing the Pleasure Horse | 9 |
| | 3 | The Value of the Bronc Pen in Training | 15 |
| | 4 | Using the Right Kind of Gear | 43 |
| | 5 | Time for the Colt's First Ride | 48 |
| | 6 | Work away from the Fence: Inside Lead | 73 |
| | 7 | Developing Correct Leads | 90 |
| | 8 | The Neck Rein and the Finishing Bit | 104 |
| | 9 | Training the Rope Horse | 110 |
| | 10 | Choosing and Training the Cutting Horse | 126 |
| | 11 | Understanding the Cutting Horse Rules | 142 |
| | 12 | Accident Prevention | 161 |
| | 13 | Handling Stallions | 171 |
| | 14 | Discipline Without Spoiling | 185 |
| | 15 | Leading, Loading, and Hauling | 197 |
| | 16 | The Hard-to-Mount Horse | 203 |
| | 17 | The Bucking Horse | 208 |
| | 18 | Kickers and Strikers | 217 |
| | 19 | Barn-Sour and Runaway Horses | 227 |
| | 20 | The Spooking, Shying Horse—The Timid Horse | 233 |
| | 21 | Tail Wringers and Head Tossers | 247 |
| | 22 | Falling Horses | 258 |
| | 23 | Some Really Tough Problems | 267 |
| | 24 | The Selection and Care of the Saddle | 277 |
| Index | | | 283 |

# Preface

I have always liked horses. I think this is a prime requisite for a horse trainer, though there seem to be a lot of horse trainers who don't like horses. If you ask me, people who are constantly clubbing the horses they're supposed to be training don't like horses. And if they have this disdain for horses, they should be in some other line of work, for they must be leading miserable lives—as are their horses.

Some trainers knock and spur a handle on their horses. That's one way. You won't find that kind of stuff in this book. Sure, sometimes you have to get a little rough with a rough horse, and I'll tell you how to do this. But I won't tell you how to beat up a horse.

I guess I should tell you about my qualifications so you can decide for yourself whether or not you want to read this book. There are a lot of horse-training books about, and the reader should be selective.

My mother foaled me in 1927 in the little town of Columbus Grove, Ohio. I had already had some riding experience, for she rode quite a bit and even did some jumping while she was carrying me. My dad had always had horses, though most were the kind you hitch to a buggy.

I can't remember the time when I didn't have a pony or a horse. But no one knew much about training a saddle horse in Columbus Grove back in those days, and most horses were a sorry-going lot.

When World War II came along, people started having some money in their pockets, and the pleasure horse came into his own. I was right among them. I got my first job breaking horses for pay in 1943, as I recall.

I really thought I was salty. Other kids were playing baseball and football; I was breaking horses. I was short on science but long on determination. Those horses ended up broke, but they were what we later called "sop and 'tater" horses. I sure couldn't teach them what I didn't know.

After serving some navy (Davy Jones, ha, ha) and college time, I headed west. I'd decided life would be a miserable thing without horses, so I'd best get on with it. I had a period of time just drifting around, trying to learn a business with no one to teach me anything.

Heck, I used to forefoot a colt, hobble him, tie up a hind foot, saddle him, slip on a hackamore, and go for a ride. I remember that I once broke fourteen colts to ride with not a one in the bunch knowing how to lead. I'd ride up to a gate, get off to open it, get on, ride through, and get off to close it.

I was riding for the Hachet Cattle Company when I met Jack Link, a California cowboy. Jack didn't like my horses or the way I handled them. He was a strong talker about what a dandy hand he was. The longer I knew him, the more he'd tell me about what he could do. He'd trained every horse on the West Coast that was worth anything. He'd worked with every top trainer. He'd doubled for all the top western movie stars and called them by their first names. He could make the best saddles, braid hackamores, engrave silver, outrope the best, and ride any bronc at any given time. My mama had told me plainly, "Self-praise stinks!" and this egomaniac really got under my hide. I was happy when the roundup ended and we went our separate ways.

That winter I got a job caretaking and breaking a few colts on a dude ranch up above Cripple Creek, Colorado. On my first trip to town I saw Jack. He'd just married a young

Cripple Creek girl and had no job or money. He asked how I was doing, and I told him that I was slowly starving to death. He said that he was in the same fix and thought he'd move in with me so we could all starve together. And I just stood there and let him move in.

Jack made a deal with a local horseman, and we soon had a hundred colts to break. Then I got quite a surprise. Jack could do what he said he could. What a hand he was! I learned more from him in two weeks than I'd learned in two years before I met him. Those colts worked in an unbelievable fashion. Jack showed me how to pick the right split second to pull a rein to slide a horse, how to double a rank one to make him pay attention, and how to make one handy by riding circles and figure eights.

He'd rope a colt while sitting on an old packhorse. His loop would snake out and throatlatch the colt. Then he'd throw some slack into the air to give himself time to dally. He'd have the colt hobbled and saddled in no time. I rode most of the colts with Jack sitting on the fence yelling at me what to do. Jack showed me that I had a lot to learn and then started teaching me. I've tried to shy away from getting a know-it-all attitude since then, for Jack humbled me for all time.

I've worked in California, Colorado, Nebraska, South Dakota, Pennsylvania, Ohio, Virginia, and now Florida. I've learned something in each of those states. In Virginia, I met the famous circus rider Arthur Konyot, who was teaching and training for Arthur Godfrey. We became good friends, and I was amazed at what his dressage horses could do. He'd talk about "collection" where the Californians would say "up in the bridle." Konyot got me more interested in aids, suppleness, and, of course, collection.

I've had my own training stables at various times, and the horses that were brought to me were a real education. You must produce results, or you don't eat. What can you do when the horse brought to you is a runaway, a bucker, a rearer, or a sulker or doesn't have any "try"? A trainer has a couple of things that he can rely on. The first is a glib tongue. I told myself early in my training career that I wouldn't use this aid. I would be honest with my clients.

If a glib tongue is rejected, the trainer must achieve results. Every horse is different. There's no set pattern for training. Every bad habit the horse has must be analyzed, and a plan must be formulated to deal with the problem. If the plan doesn't work, the trainer must find one that will. He must go for results. A plan that works on one horse may or may not work on another horse with similar bad habits. This kind of scheming about how to outwit the bad-habit horse is constant, but very rewarding for the person who really wants to learn the training business.

Knowledge of horses can be ours by observing. We can watch the best trainers in the business and learn from them. We can figure out a lot for ourselves. If we're advised to use a certain rig for a particular horse, we can try to figure out why. If we find no answers by questions and observations, we turn to the written word.

Of course, no book can be a substitute for personal experience. The old cowboy who learned by riding the rough string really learned and could afford to be scornful of the book-learned horseman. But a book can be a shortcut to information that you haven't gotten around to experiencing yet. When I started as a trainer, I'd have given a lot for a book like this one to ease me over some of the rough spots. I've had many a hard knock learning some of the things I've put in this book.

*Dave Jones*

*Monticello, Florida*

# PRACTICAL WESTERN TRAINING

# 1. What to Look for in a Horse

BACK in the early 1950s, I worked for Charles G. Araujo, of, Coalinga, California. He produced winning horses and showed the foundation of a big, popular branch of Quarter Horses that have gone on to make up the cutting and reining horse bloodlines of today. His conformation horses also performed in working events where such events are very difficult to win—California. When he was asked what he looked for in a top horse, he gave a stock one-word answer: "Conformation." He was right. If you have superior conformation, you have everything. You even have brains, for I've never seen a stupid horse that had a good head.

Styles come and go. The horse with superior conformation might not be the halter winner of the moment, but a good horse is a good horse. He'll have his day, and conformation will win out in the long run.

Let's start with the head. It should go with the body, being just the right size to fit the rest of the horse. The forehead should be flat, with good width between the eyes. The eyes should be large and brown and have the appearance of superior intelligence and kindness. I don't like white showing around the eyes, but we have to excuse this in Appaloosas and, perhaps, Paints. Ears should be small and set well up on the head. Width between eyes and ears denotes brain room.

The muzzle should be small, and the mouth should be narrow. The little muzzle should swell to a powerful jaw. This is emphasized more in a stallion than in a mare. The neck should be fairly long. It's almost impossible for a horse to flex properly with a short, stubby neck. The throatlatch should be refined and neat. An "upside-down neck" is undesirable. This condition is called "ewe neck." Any horse with this type neck will be high-headed and much more difficult to get a good head-set on.

The gelding and mare should never have cresty, stallion-type necks. The stallion gets more and more neck through the years. The mare should have a feminine appearance.

I like medium withers, high enough to keep a saddle from slipping but not so high as to rub the fork of the saddle. The low-withered horse is said to have "mutton withers." Avoid this if possible, for the saddle will have to be pulled and kept very tight on such a horse.

The shoulder line influences head carriage. A sloping shoulder, such as is common with Arabians and Thoroughbreds, means that the head will be carried high—proud. The working-type Quarter Horse has a steeper shoulder line, so the normal head carriage is lower.

The girth of a horse is important. He should "cinch up big" so he has plenty of heart and lung room.

The underline is also very important to the working horse and means "depth through the loin." If a horse cuts up steeply from the cinch to the flank, he has little depth through the loin. Such horses look like greyhounds. This is all right in the long-distance racehorse, but is undesirable in horses that work off the hind legs.

One thing we see too much of today is the high-rumped horse. When a horse with a rump six inches higher than his withers works well, it's the exception rather than the rule. The high-rumped horse will appear to have long legs behind and short ones up front.

When you notice pleasure horses in a show, you'll see a number of them traveling slightly on two-tracks (that is,

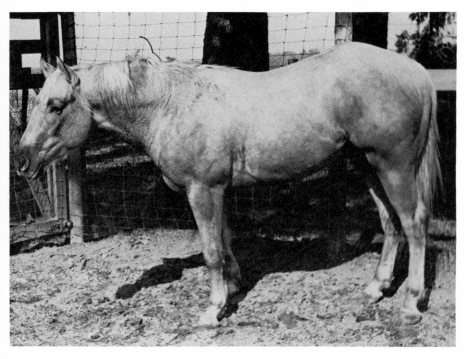

One thing we see too much of is the high-rumped horse.

moving forward and to one side at the same time), with heads out and quarters in. If you were to check their conformation when they're unsaddled, you'd see that they are higher at the croup than at the withers. Such horses invariably two-track when going just the slightest bit downhill. To straighten them out, you have to teach them to work on two-tracks. This gives you enough control so that you can use leg aids to make them travel straight.

Notice a horse with a high rump going uphill, working on the level, and then going a little bit downhill. He'll travel straight going uphill, will be somewhat straight on the level,

5

but will two-track going downhill. You can help such a horse by getting all possible weight off his back and onto the stirrups. This is very observable.

I like quite a bit of slope to the croup, with the tail set low between the buttocks. I don't like a prominent tailbone that stands up over the back like a pipe. There should be a cleft down the rump deep enough to "hold dust." The slope of the croup allows the horse to get his hind legs up under him when he is stopping and turning.

A horse should have good depth of hip—the length from the flank to the point of the butt. This means power in his propelling force, the hindquarters.

Hind legs should be in correct alignment and neither too straight nor too crooked, for infirmities are inherent with either fault. An imaginary line running along the back tendon from fetlock to hock should just touch the point of the butt. This holds true only if the horse's hooves are properly trimmed and he's standing straight. A long toe will make the horse appear crooked-legged. The hoof should have approximately the same angle as the pastern.

Bone should be adequate to support the horse's bulk. Don't buy a horse whose legs appear too refined. Very small bone spells trouble in the long run.

There should be a definite separation between cannon bone and tendon. You've heard horsemen say that a horse has "good flat bone." A horse has no flat bones in his legs. But when the tendon stands well out from the cannon bone, the appearance is sort of flat. The horse whose tendon lies close to the bone looks and is "tied in at the knees" in front and appears too delicate behind.

The cannon bone should sit under the knee in the front legs. This gives the horse a slightly knock-kneed appearance, but it's correct. Some horses' cannon bones are set too far out, giving a straight-legged appearance. This is a weakness called "bench knees" and is very bad.

When viewing the horse from the rear we should see greater width at the stifle than at the hips. This means power and ability to work off the hind legs. The gaskin muscle should be fairly even and show almost as much on the inside as on the outside. A horse with no inside gaskin muscle will wear down his hooves on the outside, with the inside surface of the hoof building up while the outside is wearing away. Uneven gaskin muscling means hoof trouble or, at least, constant hoof attention.

The horse's toes should point straight ahead. Constant hoof trimming can often improve or correct crookedness, but he's a better colt if this isn't necessary (lower the outside of the hoof if he toes out; lower the inside if he toes in; results are instantly observed). Toeing out is a worse fault than toeing in and is harder to correct.

One must be very careful when trimming or shoeing to correct toe in or out. You can help a little, but don't overdo it. It's best to level the hoof and then check by watching how the horse puts his hooves down when he walks. We check this on hard-packed sand. If the hoof twists when it hits, it needs more trimming. If he toes out and twists out at a walk, take a little more off the outside. If the hoof hits flat, leave it alone.

If you trim a horse whose legs (look carefully at the knees) point out, the hooves should point out at the same angle. If you trim a colt in until his hooves point straight ahead while his conformation says he should toe out, you'll lame him.

No discussion of conformation is complete without considering conformation under saddle. The horse should appear alert but not jumpy. He should travel with his nose in—

never out like a pointer dog. The neck should flex, giving a proud appearance. The tail should be carried gracefully, out from the butt. Sometimes a horse that one might overlook in the pasture will look brilliant under saddle.

Most important of all, the whole horse should always appear to fit together in correct proportion. Different breeds and types may vary somewhat in their special characteristics, but a good horse is a good horse, and if you're lucky enough to own one, learn to do right by him!

# 2. Developing the Pleasure Horse

I couldn't begin to count the times I've been asked the question, "Where can I find a gentle, young, good-looking western horse for my family?" There are plenty of average horses around, but the true pleasure horse is hard to find. Yet I believe that the gentle, well-adjusted pleasure horse is really the mainstay of any breed of horses. The really marketable equine is the gentle horse that a beginner can hack around on in safety and yet not be ashamed to ride. No novice will stick with horses long enough to become proficient if his first horse jerks away and kicks at him with malice aforethought.

Horses are so different that it's almost impossible to set up standards to ensure that a gentle, well-behaved animal will result. I think, however, that those who breed and raise horses can take a big step forward by following this formula:

The dam should be gentle—the spook will raise a spook. The sire should be a working horse that has shown successfully. It's hard to show a silly horse and a pleasure to show a well-mannered one.

The kind, intelligent mother will care for her offspring twenty-four hours a day. She will warn him about things he should fear and instill confidence in him when he should be unafraid. If a man walks into the pasture and the mother flees in terror, the colt will have fear of man instilled in him. If the colt sees that mother walks up to a man to have her back scratched, the colt will also be unafraid.

The breeder should thoroughly acquaint himself with the

colt during the preweaning period. If he can get the colt to come to him for feeding and grooming, he's on the right track. The colt should be caught and led. If time is allowed for this, fighting will be kept to a minimum. The colt's confidence in the human will grow.

At weaning time the colt's world explodes. The day he is taken from his mother is the worst day of his life. He's inconsolable. The human can't help him except by leaving him alone. However, the old saying "Misery loves company" is very true. Two or more colts should be kept together at weaning time if at all possible.

Soon after weaning, the colts should be separated from the fillies. This is when colts learn to be buddies. They form friendships that are very strong. As with humans, this is a time for fighting, and buddies will stick together to fight other colts, like the wild kids who roam the streets of big cities looking for a "rumble." These little spats are natural for young horses and are a part of growing up.

Yet this is a time when colts can learn to be wild. Close human association is very desirable. In practice most colts are turned out to shift for themselves until the time comes for them to be broken. If time is allotted to handle these younger colts, the results will be well worth the effort. They can be led, have their hooves trimmed, be longed, or even be driven. Handling will pay off in making the colt a gentler horse. Too much longeing is, I believe, a poor practice; making a colt travel round and round puts excessive wear on his joints. Once in a while is enough. A person will watch how hard colts play and think that such a statement is silly—but the colt doesn't go round and round while playing. He's all over the place. That is better for him.

Deviating too much from the normal isn't wise. The colt should grow up in a pasture with colts his own age to develop a good horse-to-horse relationship. Raising the colt

The pastured colt may get a few lumps and scratches from his buddies, but he'll be much healthier mentally.

in a stall with humans as his only companions is unhealthy. If he's in a pasture with his kind, he'll be gentler with other horses. We've all seen box-stall-raised horses that want to kick every other horse in sight. The colt in the pasture may get a few lumps and scratches from his buddies, but he'll be much healthier mentally.

When training time comes, the degree of gentleness, how he feels about humans, past experiences, breeding, and handling will all determine whether he will be a reliable pleasure

11

We're pleased with the colt, and he's pleased with us.

horse or a "cowboy's" horse. There are only a few cowboys, but there are a lot of green riders who would like something they can feel safe with.

Training boils down to *punishment* and *reward.* By punishment I don't mean getting wild-eyed, foaming at the mouth, and beating the horse with a chain or a two-by-four. Punishment means a rap with a whip, calmly and immediately carried out as a result of a colt's mistake. Punishment is a yell or a growl. Punishment is a rap with the lead rope when the colt is unruly. Punishment must be immediate, or the horse can't associate it with his bad action. It shouldn't terrorize the colt. It shouldn't instill a long-remembered fear or hate. The colt should have and show affection for his trainer if he's to be a pleasure horse.

If a colt makes a major mistake, such as kicking you, punish him, but don't loose fury upon him. Punishment for doing something bad is retribution. The same punishment accompanied by fury is a very different thing and will terrorize a colt. Punishment administered with love will never terrorize a horse.

Reward means a kind word, a tidbit, a pat on the neck, a chance to stand and get normal breathing back, loosening the cinch, or airing the back on a hot day. A reward is almost anything we do to show the colt that he's done a good job and that we're pleased with him.

Training should proceed in an orderly manner, one thing at a time. A good horse may result from hurried training, but chances for success are greatly enhanced if proper time is allotted to each phase of training.

All this takes patience. Yet if I'm asked what question I hear the most as a horse trainer, I'd have to say this: "How long will it take?"

I get this question even from ol' boys who should know better. Of course, my answer is always in the form of a question: "What do you want the colt to do, and how well do you want him to do it?"

The more you handle horses, the more you should realize how little you actually know. A trainer who wants to be a good one will learn something every day from his horses.

There are trainers who can have a colt really percolating in a month or two. The novice horse owner may be impressed by this, but the horses won't be. They'll fear a human. Most any trainer can knock and spur a handle on a colt in thirty days. But the colt has nowhere to go but downhill. Who in the world wants a horse he has to beat up to get him to work?

A good colt should be trained slow and easy. If trained right, he'll retain what he learns and will always be a good horse. A horse shouldn't dread being ridden. He should enjoy it.

Sure, horses will work if trained by rough, crude methods. A cutting horse might make the top ten with some "tiger" always knocking on him. But most horses made this way are mediocre and no pleasure to handle. A horse will do a better job, work correctly, and be friendly if he's had good sensible training. Anyone can brainwash a horse. Not everyone can train one.

# 3. The Value of the Bronc Pen in Training

PEOPLE often write or call about problems they've come up against with colts they've started. They've read, watched, and had some experience—enough that they thought they could do their own training. Usually their equipment and facilities weren't suitable for starting colts. Their knowledge and experience were far too skimpy.

We have two bronc pens and three arenas. One bronc pen and an arena are under huge live-oak trees. We use this setup during our summers, when riding in the sun is too hot for horses and men.

The bronc pens are fifty feet square and eight feet high. When people see these high fences, they ask what kind of wild ones we handle here. The high fences discourage broncs from trying to jump out.

A few years ago I was building a bronc pen. A two-year-old colt wandered into the pen from the arena. I'd just stretched a five-foot-high length of woven wire and was getting ready to add my wooden planks. I looked at him. He was full of beans and silly. Acting like a bronc, he tried to jump out. He hit the fence about four feet high and gave it a bad stretching. The fence was a foot off the ground, so he actually tried to clear six feet.

No matter how carefully or scientifically you carry a colt along in his preride days, he may blow the plug during his first few rides. A high fence is security against hurting him or getting hurt by him.

I actually see more colts wanting to buck today than I saw

The high bronc-pen fences discourage broncs from trying to jump out. Alan Dewey on the bronc.

thirty years ago. They are more spirited, and they're fed much more potent feed. I don't think a grass-fed four-year-old is as apt to buck or do other silly things as a big stout two-year-old who's been fed high-potency grain right from the start.

Bronc pens are usually built small enough that a colt can't really get up a head of steam whether tied up or running. A forty-foot-square pen is fine if you're starting small, handy colts. The fifty-foot square is better for all-around

I see more colts wanting to buck today than I saw thirty years ago. David Baggett on a bronc.

use. If you have to rope one once in a while, he can't drag you all over the pasture in a small pen.

Many people object to having their horses roped. If the roper knows what he's doing, it's often a good thing. A gentle colt will sometimes feel so silly he won't allow his handler to walk up to him. Rather than rant and rave when

17

this happens, I just get a lariat and rope the colt. If I turn him out in a lot or pasture, I want to know I can catch him. When I'm not sure, I turn him loose in the bronc pen. If you try to rope him in a lot, chances are he'll get spooked and try to jump out. Roping's OK if you use your head.

Last year an Arabian gelding was hauled to me. He had been hard to break and was still snappy. His owner took him for a long trail ride and didn't realize that the cinch was loose. The horse, Dorze, spooked, and the saddle turned, throwing the rider. It was weeks before they managed to catch the terrified gelding. He'd kicked the saddle apart, but the fright remained.

The owner had several girls on his staff who were Meredith Manor honor graduates, but Dorze was too rank for them. He'd kick. Trying to ride him was inviting disaster, so they shipped him to me. The girls cautioned me about his kicking.

The first morning he was here, we took Dorze to the bronc pen and turned him loose. When I tried to walk up to him, he wheeled his rear toward me and set himself to kick.

Many trainers would get a whip and try to whip-break such a horse. I've seen many horses turned into man haters by overuse of the whip, so I took another route, I picked up a lariat and went back to the horse.

As I approached him, he wheeled to kick. When I lifted the loop, he ran by me, and I roped him around the neck. Dorze bellowed, bucked, and reared. I took a hip lock on the rope, dug in the heels, and turned him to face me. When I'd stopped him, I immediately loosened the lariat so he wouldn't be choked down.

When I walked toward him, he turned, but I jerked him around and slowly approached. The rollers in his nose snorted a warning, so I took care to veer off rather than go straight

Ranald Cameron, my Australian apprentice, climbing all over a hobbled-and-sidelined bronc.

at his head, for a horse, unlike a gun, can fire with both ends.

When I reached him, I crooned some sweet, low words and scratched his neck. When he seemed to be enjoying that stuff, I pulled the lariat from his neck. He took off. When I walked toward him, he wheeled to kick. I roped him again.

19

All this was repeated until I'd roped him six times. After that, he followed me around the pen like a well-trained puppy dog.

We eventually cured this horse of his fear under saddle. He was hobbled and sidelined in the pen. When he found that he couldn't escape or fight, he stood. His rider would crawl all over him. One Australian apprentice even ran up behind and vaulted into the saddle. Of course, the horse was restrained during all this. We showed the gelding much affection—no whips—and he responded in time.

I consider the bronc pen vital. My riders soon learn that it's one of the best helpers they have. In fact, they want to stay in it too long, for a colt has to turn so much in a small pen that he soon thinks that's all there is to a ride. When given more room, he travels like a snake, looking to turn this way or that. A few rides in the big arena take care of this problem.

I've said nothing about training colts to stand tied. Why not? Because it's too easy to untrain one. You can teach a colt to stand tied, but someone will do something to startle him. He'll fly back, break loose, and immediately become a halter puller. However:

A good snubbing post should be used for colt training. If you tie to a fence, you have less than a 180-degree escape route; with a post, you have 360 degrees.

The post should be at least six feet high out of the ground, for a colt may jump on a short post and hurt himself. A notch is cut in the post so the rope can't slip down. We tie a soft foot rope around the colt's neck and run the rope through the halter. The pull is back far enough that the colt won't injure himself. To really retrain a bad puller, tie an inner tube on a tall post and fasten the rope to the tube.

A rope running around the horse's cinch area, between his legs and up through the halter may work, but it makes

Ray Liss giving a colt his first ride. Glenn Lillibridge is helping on the ground. Note the high-notched snubbing post in the foreground.

a horse so sore he can't be saddled for weeks. This method is fine for weanlings.

Never, never, never tie up a horse and leave him alone. Always be nearby, and always have a sharp knife on hand. He may fight, fall, hang, and die if left alone.

The snubbing post in the bronc pen is a hindrance as well as a help. When you are starting a colt, he may hit it, hurt himself, or come so close to it he makes you hit it. For those who have the space and money, I suggest having

21

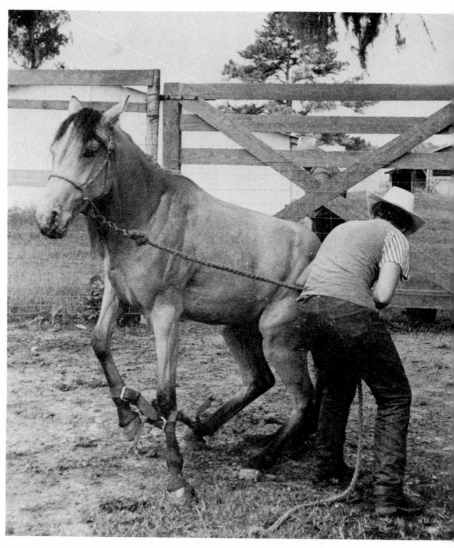

Lillibridge trying to handle the hooves of a hobbled-and-sidelined bronc.

an extra pen—say forty feet square—with a good stout snubbing post in it. If you raise horses and have a lot of colts to work, you need a snubbing post.

Most horses that come here for retraining have broken loose and are halter pullers. We do nothing about this unless specifically instructed to teach the horse to stand tied.

Unless otherwise instructed, we train colts to hobbles and sideline. I've devised a special piece of hardware that makes the sideline practical. Fastening a sideline to front hobbles soon wrecks most hobbles on the market, so I came up with this rig that doesn't put a twist on the hobble rig when used.

Is it necessary? When handling stallions, this rig eases the problem of washing the genitals before and after breeding. It makes saddling a cinch. It helps teach a colt not to fight if he gets tangled up in wire. When used with a double sideline, it's unbeatable as a breeding hobble. I trust this rig and don't trust regular breeding hobbles.

When you are ironing out spoiled horses, hobbles and sideline are invaluable, for you have control over a horse without hitting him. About all he can do to injure a person is fall on him.

We never try to train a horse to front hobbles without the sideline, for doing so just teaches a horse to run when hobbled. He can still kick and strike. After initial training, he can be hobbled for saddling without the sideline, and we use a soft, braided hobble for this.

The gentle horse is easy to hobble and sideline. We just got a nice young spoiled gelding in to reform. Same old story. The saddle came loose and got under him. Next time they tried to saddle him, he bucked and ran away. The owner thought she had a real problem.

This horse, Rafe, is a gentle soul. We hobbled and sidelined him in the bronc pen and then got away to let him figure it out for himself. We moved back but didn't leave the scene, for we wanted to be there to help him if he fell and couldn't get up.

Rafe tested the rig. He almost fell. "Whoops! Better stand and think this out. Move foot a little. Can't move. OK, I'll stand."

Wayne, an apprentice, brought up a saddle blanket. Rafe snorted. Wayne gave him a piece of carrot. He placed the blanket on Rafe's back. All's well. Next came the saddle. Rafe moved around a little but remembered the hobbles and sideline. The saddle was cinched up. The hackamore was put on his head and adjusted for size. The *mecate* (hair reins and lead rope) was tied up in the proper position. Hobbles and sideline were removed. Rafe walked off. No problem. Dan, my other apprentice, mounted and rode the gelding. Rafe was gentle but knew nothing.

The next day Rafe was hobbled and sidelined. After Rafe was saddled, Dan rigged him to drive and gave it a try. Rafe kept turning, wanting to face Dan. Before long he drove pretty well.

The next day Dan drove Rafe before riding him. He managed to get Rafe backing up while being driven but didn't try this from the saddle for, say, a week. We had the colt going well before the owner even expected us to ride him.

OK, you say, Rafe was gentle. How the heck do you hobble and sideline a wild one?

The experienced trainer has many tools at his disposal. If the colt can be led and handled a bit, he can probably be blindfolded. We make a blindfold by cutting up an old blanket. It should be about twenty-four inches square. A six-inch slit is cut in the center for the colt's ears. A loop and a tie string are sewn at the border of the blindfold directly down from the slit.

Slip the blindfold over the colt's head, passing it over the

Bill Coleman and Ken Serco handling a blindfolded colt.

ears. Tie it down. He may jerk around and snort a little, but he should soon stand. Go all over him with the hands. Before long he should accept this without flinching or moving. Go ahead. Hobble and sideline him. Remove the blindfold. Get back and let him figure it out for himself. Do this in a bronc pen with a soft base—sand or soft dirt. If he should fall with his head under him, straighten him out immediately. Most will hop around a little but will soon stand. Reward him with a tidbit or at least kind words and friendly pats.

25

Fay with one leg scotch-hobbled.

Can't get a blindfold on him? OK, scotch up a hind leg first: Tie a soft rope, about twenty to twenty-five feet long, around his neck with a bowline knot. Flip a loop of this rope so that it lies before a hind foot. Lead him into the loop. Pull it up and tie it off with a couple of half hitches. He'll fight it a little. If it doesn't come off, lift the hoof by hand and take a turn of the rope around it. He can't kick much or fight. Go ahead and gentle him. Handle his legs when you think it's safe. Hobble and sideline him.

Still can't get it done? Use two scotch hobbles. Scotch up one leg. Start to scotch up the other leg. When you pull

Fay with both legs scotch-hobbled.

the second scotch rope, the colt will sit down like a dog. Tie off the rope. Push him over. You can now easily hobble and sideline him. Take off the scotch-hobble ropes and let him up. Go ahead and handle him to get him gentle.

If he's a totally wild bronc, you can't scotch-hobble him. Drive him into the bronc pen. If you can't rope, get someone who can. Forefoot and bust him. Keep the rope tight. Have someone put a knee on his neck and raise his nose. Hobble and sideline him. Let him up and gentle him.

You can't rope? OK, let's try the good ol' Jeffery method of horse control.

27

Some Australian folks interested in our way of training in the United States liked my material and started corresponding with me. They sent me several Australian books on training. One was *The Jeffery Method of Horse Handling,* by Maurice Wright. I didn't pay much attention to it at the time.

Then came Filly. This little "bronca" wasn't playing with a full deck. Her mother was stupid, and her daughters inherited the trait.

Filly had been turned out with a Johnson rope halter on her. Then her owners couldn't catch her. The halter grew into her head. When the people got close enough to her to see what kind of shape she was in, they organized the neighborhood to pen her up and get her into a stall. They finally forced her to hold still by the might of numbers and surgically cut the halter out of her head. She was kept in a stall until she was in good enough shape to haul to me.

I had to forefoot Filly to get her sidelined and hobbled. When I tried to halter her, she nearly wiped me out by wildly flinging her head. We'd blindfold, hobble, and sideline her to put a hackamore on her. The hackamore had to be taken apart, put way back, and gradually brought up into position. She hit all of us in the face—*hard*—at one time or another.

As time passed, Filly went well under saddle, but she had that one great problem about her head. Nothing helped. I had a month to go before she went home, and I was getting desperate.

As I was passing the bookcase, the book from Australia caught my eye. I skimmed through it and, being desperate, tried Jeffery's "magic longe." Damned if it didn't work. The filly stood like a statue while I put the full *jáquima con fiador* over her ears time and time again. I was amazed.

The only thing I did to get this amazing response was to

put a rope around her neck. When she thought about flinging her head, I jerked and released the rope. Period.

*How* did it work? *Why* did it work?

I believe that a horse, like a person, can really concentrate on only one thing at a time. If I'm writing an article
and have a country-music tape on the stereo, I either can't
concentrate on the article or can't concentrate on the music.
If the article is something I'm really interested in doing, the
music is nearly blocked out.

In this fashion I can be making a saddle in the shop with
the TV on. When work gets to the point where I have to
concentrate on it, the TV is blacked out. I try to schedule
the hand sewing I do when there's something on TV I want
to watch, for I can do hand sewing without thinking about it.

This is why the Jeffery rope (and war bridles) work. A
horse thinks about kicking you. Then a rope pulls on the
neck. The horse must think about the rope pulling the neck
rather than the kicking. In this way a colt can easily be
taught to stand for hoof trimming and shoeing.

Few men can work a war bridle without flying off the
handle and overdoing it. The horse then associates pain with
shoeing or whatever else is to be accomplished. The Jeffery
rope produces the same results while the temptation to cause
pain is mostly removed. The rope is *always* released after
it's pulled.

This method is used in Australia by a few people to break
wild range colts in a couple of hours. Maurice Wright wrote
the book about the Jeffery method. He gives exhibitions of
this, turning a raw untamed colt into a gentle ridable colt
in two hours.

Jeffery and Wright don't believe in roping their pupils.
Rather, they place the lariat over the colt's head by laying
the rope out on a long tree branch and draping it on after
the colt is cornered in a small pen. Or they have a rider

Start of the Jeffery series. Bill Levitz has the control rope on a pole and is slipping up to the colt.

Opposite top: Bill has slipped the loop over the colt's head and is pulling the pole away.

Opposite bottom: The colt wheels and runs away. Bill runs to keep up and tries to pull the colt around to face him.

Bill has the colt pretty well stopped. He'll release his tight hold on the rope and use pulls and releases. Jeffrey would sometimes take a dally on a post after he noosed the colt.

Opposite top: The colt stands quietly while Bill handles the front hooves.

Opposite bottom: The colt continues to stand while the hind hooves are handled.

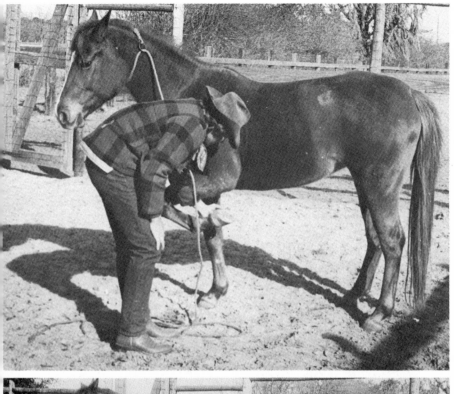

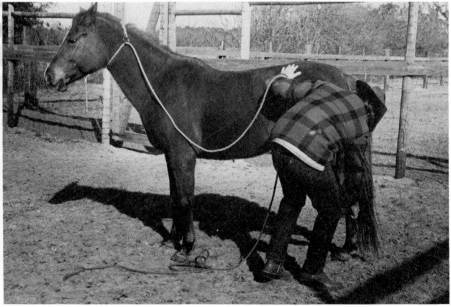

Bill has gone all over the colt with his hands. Now he carefully eases onto the colt's back.

Bill now eases his right leg across the colt.

Bill slides off the colt's rump.

Opposite top: Bill saddles the colt.

Opposite bottom: The colt is allowed to move away from his handler. He spooks and runs. A sharp jerk on the rope will have him under control.

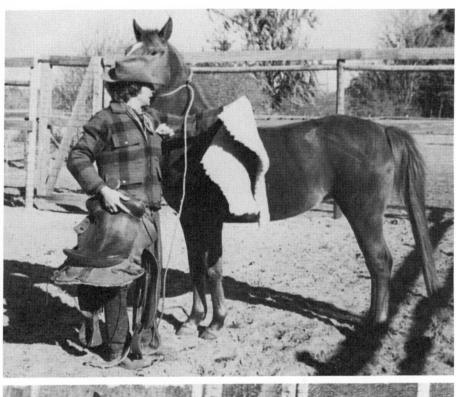

Lillibridge is to give the colt his first ride. The colt seems to shut his eyes so he won't see what's going on. (Actually, the camera just caught him blinking.)

place the loop for them. They feel that roping the colt and *missing* him might frighten him.

Being a roper, I don't feel that way. Of course, I seldom miss. I don't swing a rope more than once before a throw at a horse, and I can catch without swinging it at all. I feel that a colt respects me when I can stretch my arm out, stop him, and make him turn and face me. At any rate, I do rope colts when I have to.

The handler simply jerks the rope when the colt tries to get away, kick, or strike. Before long the handler goes over

The colt flurries a bit but soon settles down to do very well for a first ride.

every place on the horse with his hands. He handles the colt's legs and picks up the hooves. He lies across the unsaddled colt and soon sits on him. He brings up the blanket and saddle. Before long he's riding the colt.

We often use the Jeffery rope for hard-to-bridle horses, horses bad about their hooves, and hard-to-mount horses. I don't use it to start colts—I don't see where we'd be ahead in the long run—or we use other methods with the Jeffery rope.

When I start a colt, I hobble and sideline him. When

39

he's saddled and has a hackamore or colt bit on him, I may longe him a little. Personally, I don't like to get into the habit of longeing horses, for I feel that we should be able to take a colt from his stall, saddle, mount, and ride away with no need to longe to get the buck out of him. Someday someone might try to ride the horse without prelongeing him and get hurt.

I like to drive colts before riding them. This doesn't go in harmony with the Jeffery method, for the latter teaches the colt to stop and face the trainer. Driving gentles the colt; the colt learns to start, stop, turn, and back up when driven. After such fine ground training, the actual riding comes as but another step in a series. I don't think time can be saved by skipping the driving step.

However, other styles develop that don't go hand in hand with driving. Some trainers advocate a Jeffery-like method whereby they gentle, mount, and let the colt go where he wants to and do what he wants to. I recently read about a trainer who starts colts with nothing whatsoever on their heads. This develops into a training procedure where the colt does what the trainer wants him to do but thinks he (the colt) is doing what he wants to do. I can't knock this for I haven't seen it work. It does seem to me that the trainer must always know what the colt is thinking. I confess that I can't do that, and I thought I knew what the mare says to the colt.

To drive the colt, we hobble the stirrups—tie a rope from one stirrup to the other under the colt's belly. It's wise to take time to raise the stirrups enough so they won't strike the colt's elbow when he's working. We use old longe lines for driving lines after tying a few knots in the driver's ends, for the nylon lines can really burn your hands.

For the first driving session it's nice to have a helper give you a hand. The colt's hobbled and sidelined while the

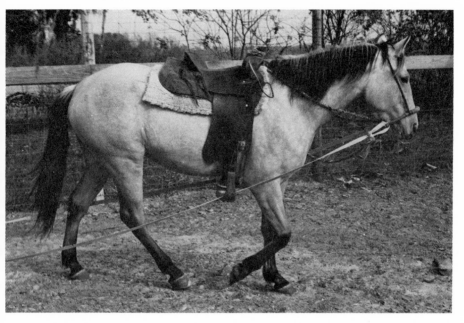

Driving the colt.

lines are run through the tied-down stirrups. Hobbles and sideline are removed. The trainer stands on one side of the colt with the helper standing on the other side. Both people take a line and walk to the rear of the colt. The helper hands his line to the trainer and then moves back to the colt to help start him moving. Often the colt must be pushed sideways to make him move his hooves. This tells him that he's no longer restrained and is free to move.

Sometimes there's quite a flurry. The colt may buck or rear when he feels the driving lines touch his rear. That is one reason I prefer a square bronc pen to a round one (though both kinds are great to have). He can be jammed into a corner if he seems too wild to run along behind. When he's stopped in the corner, he can be made to stand until he's calmed down. When restarted, he can be turned into the next corner if he continues his wild ways. Before long he'll be driving in fine fashion.

Some colts drive well from the start. A few will explode wildly, jerk away, and get the lines crossed under them. If it appears dangerous to try to get up to such a colt to straighten out the mess, I'll just rope him and start over. By roping him, I again assert the fact that I'm the boss. Being able to rope has gotten me out of more messes than I can recollect, and I ask any young person who wants to be a trainer to practice roping skills until proficient.

When the colt handles fairly well, he can be asked to back. I drive him into a corner, stop him, and exert a little give-and-take pressure on the lines. The pull is so low, it's easy for the colt to tuck his head and back. I use a loud hiss for a vocal signal. The colt should be driven long enough for him to back lightly when cued by rein and vocal command.

We use vocal commands during the driving. We cluck or say "Giddap" to start. We say "Walk," "Trot," and "Whoa" when we ask for these actions. If the colt's driven two weeks, he's picking up these vocal signals.

# 4. Using the Right Kind of Gear

BEFORE going into the riding part, I want to talk a bit about gear. We use the California hackamore, a braided rawhide noseband. The good ones are braided over rawhide or over a nylon core or have no core at all. A good starting hackamore should never be braided over cable, for the cable makes it too heavy. The cable-core hackamore can't be shaped, and shaping the new hackamore to fit a horse's nose is vital to proper training. I use a piece of three-inch post for this. The back is tied in—the post is pushed down and tied in—and the sides are tied in to conform to the shape of the area where the hackamore sits. The tied hackamore is soaked overnight and dried out a few days. A good saddle soap is rubbed raw into the hackamore.

People away from the West Coast call a hackamore *(já-quima)* a *bosal.* Both mean "noseband" in Spanish. The iron-leverage kinds should be designated "mechanical hackamores." However, we have hackamore classes for young reining horses. I never heard of a "bosal class."

I've worked on the West Coast and am a little fussy about terminology. To me the hackamore is a rawhide noseband one-half inch or more in diameter complete with headstall and rein. The smaller rawhide noseband is a bosal. The pencil-size bands that go under the bridle are *bosalitos* ("little bosals").

The reins and lead rope consist of a twenty-two-foot mane-hair or mohair rope called a *mecate* (pronounced "meh-kah-tay"). The rope is tied on the hackamore so that the length

43

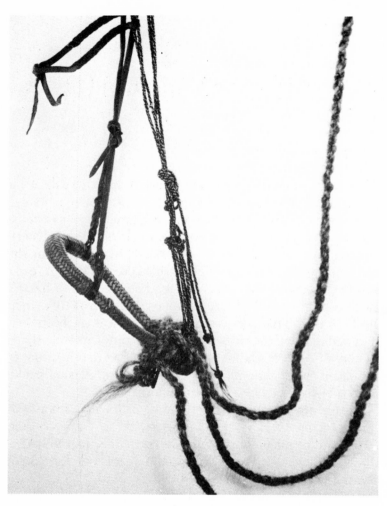

California hackamore with fiador (throatlatch) and mecate (reins and lead).

of the reins suits the rider. The rest of the rope is tied to the saddle and is used as a lead rope.

The throatlatch used with the hackamore is called a *fiador* ("fee-ah-door"). In Spanish the gear would be called *jáquima con* ("with") *fiador*. When a fiador isn't used, the reins are tied up around the neck so that the hackamore won't pull off when the colt is led or tied.

I prefer starting colts in the hackamore, though few other trainers do so. When we must pull the colt a lot, I'd rather pull on his nose than on his mouth. Some colts just won't hackamore, and when we notice this, we use the colt bit.

Why won't a colt hackamore? Some colts have such peculiar conformations of head and shoulder set that any hackamore pull skins them up. It's impossible to pad a hackamore enough to protect their jaws. Obviously it's easier to bit such a colt. Fortunately these colts are few and far between.

Some colts aren't mentally fit to hackamore. They can pull a freight train with their noses but are fairly light in the bit. Obviously there's no use trying to hackamore such a colt. All of this should be observed and acted upon right from the start.

Many trainers who eventually hackamore colts start in the colt bit. This surprised me when I worked in California, for I'd digested lore written by Luis Ortega and others about the traditional way to do things. Part of this has to do with the big, powerful colts they ride. The colts are high-lifed from the excellent California feed, and the trainer has to be continuously circling, doubling, and tucking until they settle down to work. Such circumstances call for perhaps trotting in deep sand for a half hour in the colt bit before the colt is settled down enough to work the hackamore sensibly. The colts Ed Connell and Luis Ortega wrote about were smaller, grass-grown colts that weren't too full of beans.

Almost all snaffle-bit horses I've seen have been ridden

Colt bit used with running martingale. The bit is equipped with an ordinary bit guard.

with a running martingale or draw reins during training. Personally, I favor a reworked mullen-mouth Pelham as a colt bit for the simple reason that a mullen mouth fits the natural curve made by the mouth and tongue and hence is easier on the colt. I buy a good Pelham and cut it down to make a D ring, curved-mouth colt bit. I also use a special bit guard we make here. It can be set to hold the bit high toward the roof of the colt's mouth during initial bitting periods when he's most prone to getting his tongue over the bit. Tightened down, it's the safest way to use draw reins. If draw reins are used on an unguarded bit, the whole bit can be pulled *completely through* the colt's mouth.

Steadily I get calls and letters from people who can't find good hackamores. There are far more people doing fine braiding than I know of, but I can list a few places where one can buy top rawhide gear. Ask:

Jack Shepard Custom Rawhide
520 S. 18th Street
Payette, Idaho 83661

Frank Shively
1500 W. Orchard Avenue
Nampa, Idaho 83651

Ray Holes Saddle Co.
Grangeville, Idaho 83530

Ash's Rawhide and Leather
Route 1, Box 6-C
Kooskia, Idaho 83539

# 5. Time for the Colt's First Ride

WHEN it's time for the colt's first ride, I take several things into consideration. First, what kind of owner does he have? Is the owner green or an old salt? What will the colt be used for?

If a completely gentled colt is needed, we'll start him that way. When I have apprentice riders, the extragentle way is easy. We feed the colt treats—say, cut-up carrots—and get him really liking us. One rider leads the colt while another rides. The rider on the ground can prevent the colt from running and bucking. More important, the rider on the ground can pet and talk to a nervous colt to calm him down. I know of no easier way to start a colt.

It's easy to tell whether the colt is afraid or is taking it all in stride. If he's calm and relaxed, there's no reason not to just go ahead and ride him. If he's afraid, the rider should dismount, pet the colt, lead him around, and try again. If the colt is still afraid, though he's relaxed and friendly at other times, he hasn't had enough preride preparation, such as brushing, sacking out, and driving. Back up and take more time, for you're influencing the colt's future life.

Perhaps the colt's going to be a reining or cutting horse. Don't abuse him, but skip a lot of the preliminaries. Don't get him too gentle at the start. Why not? You may take the snap out of him. The wilder colt is usually more snappy than the extremely gentle one. He's alert. He watches humans, for he hasn't lost all fear of them.

Many West Coast reinsmen hardly gentle a colt at all.

They handle him a little bit, hobble and sideline him, sack him out, and then ride. Should we feel sorry for the colt that's treated in such a fashion? No, not really. They're making reined cowhorses and need the quick response they get from colts that are a little leery of men.

If the trainer is told to make a reining horse out of a certain colt and that colt is slow to turn and stop (doggy) because he's ultragentle, the trainer will have to put some fear in him. Personally, I'd rather work a colt that has respect for me than one who walks all over me. As a general rule a trainer has to be more severe with an ultragentle colt than one that's a little wilder. I'd rather be nice than mean. Trainers often refer to gentle, friendly, doggy colts as "backyard pets."

When the colt accepts the rider, normal hackamore or snaffle-bit training proceeds. Since the colt bit is handled almost exactly like the hackamore, I won't refer to it except in a special section about the bit and guard we use.

During the first few rides the rider will use a fairly narrow rein, for the wide rein means that the hands will be well out by the colt's face, and this would probably spook the colt on his first few rides. After he develops some confidence in his rider, the low wide rein will be used.

At first the trainer is simply trying to get along with the colt and get him used to being ridden. If the colt misbehaves—bucks or runs—he's "doubled," or turned right around in his tracks.

Strength and timing are needed to double a colt correctly. He's pulled right around in a hard 180-degree turn. He should be doubled from the lowest hand position possible. A high double will pull the colt's head way up and will peel hide off his jaw.

Timing is important, for the colt should be doubled when his front hooves are leaving the ground. If the timing is

The colt should be doubled from the lowest hand position possible.

wrong, he'll have to be pulled two or more times to get him turned around.

The double is the hackamore control. When you double, you show the colt that you can turn him, control him. Do it wrong, and you show him that you can't control him, that he can buck or stampede at will.

The hackamore reins are always loose. If you try to work from a snug rein, the colt will simply take his head away from you. When you pull from a slack rein, his reaction time is too far behind your reaction time for him to set his neck rigid against your pull. If he does decide to set his neck, there's nothing to set it against, for the reins are again slack. He can't stay rigid all the time. He has to relax his neck and body so the next pull will again be against the relaxed head and neck and body.

Some colts have such thick, powerful necks that a normal person can't double them. If this is the case, don't try twice. That's what draw reins are for.

The colt speeds up. His rider wants him to slow down, so he pulls straight back on one rein and then releases it. No soap. The colt keeps going or tries to speed up. The rider should double the colt. After being doubled one way, the colt may try to run again. He should be doubled the other way, or until he responds to the slow-down or stop signals. Remember, the shoe clerk doubles high; the caballero doubles low.

I think we ride more "all over the colt" here than anywhere else. The exaggerated positions in the saddle spell out massive cues to the young horses. It looks very sloppy, but it's very effective. With weight-shift cues the colt will learn more in two weeks than he would in two months with straight-up riding.

The low wide rein. When pulling a colt as one would to circle, the rider leans forward and over far enough that he could actually pat the colt's face. He takes the hackamore rein about sixteen inches from the colt's face and pulls out to the side. When the colt's head is pulled in, the pull is released. Pull, release, pull, release. The pull lasts no more than a second. The next pull comes when needed.

When the colt is pulled the other direction, the weight shift is great—an unmistakable cue. The pull is much like pulling to lead in a certain direction. Before long the colt learns to turn into the hand, and the pulls can be very light.

Some years ago I was asked to do a combined dressage-western clinic as the western end of it. A young, spoiled filly wearing a hackamore was ridden into the arena. She halted, ran sideways, and was finally stopped by the fence.

I walked over and slipped my hackamore on her. After mounting, I used the low wide rein to move her up before the audience. As always, I rode all over her. Before long I explained my actions to the audience.

"Notice how I lead her around with those low, wide on-and-off pulls. She's following my hand with almost no pull on the reins."

With that I dropped the reins and continued leading and going through the motions with my hands. The filly responded as though I were still pulling the reins. I received a standing ovation, which frightened the filly. I went for those reins like Wes Hardin going for his six-shooter.

After the first few rides, in which a rein is held in each hand, the rider should hold the reins in the middle and move one hand down the rein to make the pull. To pull to the right, the rider centers the reins with the left hand and uses the right hand to reach down to take the rein. Vice versa for a left pull. This is a very catty way to handle the reins.

The hackamore rider must learn to handle the reins handily, Take stopping, for instance. You stop with a pull straight back, as low as possible, with one rein, holding the other rein ready in case the colt's nose pops up. If it does, you bring it down with the second rein, using a seesaw motion.

Let's say that in circling to the right you've allowed the colt to drift near the fence. You have the reins centered in your left hand. Change hands fluidly. With the reins centered in the right hand, reach forward with the left hand, grasp the rein, and pull straight back. Drop the center hold and catch the right rein with the right hand. The colt pops his nose up (the left rein has been released). Pull back on the right rein to bring the colt's nose down and in. He's still stopping. Relax the right rein, and pull the left one again. Release.

## CUES

A person who's coming right along with his or her riding and training may ask the master trainer what *specific* aids (cues) to use. The master trainer might sum it all up simply by saying, "Use what works."

For instance, when a colt has been ridden a few weeks, I might want to start teaching him how to roll back over his hocks. There are a number of signals I'd ordinarily give the colt.

We are going down the fence line and are four or five feet out from it. I will rise in the saddle seat and grab the colt with both legs. This should surprise him. Now I add a straight pull back with the rein on the fence side, let's say the left side. I'll start toward the fence at a 45-degree angle. Rein and leg pressure are released. By standing in the stirrups, I throw my weight forward, off his back. When I feel his back end drop, I know that this has happened.

I now sit down and lean back to help hold the colt's back legs in position. When his front hooves hit the ground, I allow the colt to pause a bit. This is the "dwell." The dwell time can vary from a split second to five seconds or five minutes.

I turn the colt to the left to make a 180-degree turn. He should be speeded up enough each time he turns so that he'll eventually throw himself around 180 degrees, a half circle, and jump out.

Ken Serco doing a rollback on the fence. He's using a right leg back of the cinch and a light paddle on the right side of the colt's neck.

If the colt is still a little leery of me, I may tap him on the leg or right side of his chest with my boot heel or stirrup. This startles him into making the 180-degree turn. Moving him out rapidly keeps speed in the turn, which is very desirable for a proper rollback. By tapping him with boot or stirrup on the right side when turning left, I've used an *outside* leg aid.

If such a cue forward of the cinch didn't work, I'd try bumping the colt with my heel just back of the cinch. It's still an outside leg cue, but my leg is in a different position. Use what works.

Remember, at the stop I was forward to allow the colt to arch his back when I grabbed him with both legs. The rider's weight should be off the seat whenever a horse needs to arch his back. Then I sat down to hold the hind legs in position. When I turn him into the fence and jump him out, I quickly get forward again. These are body-weight cues, and they are very important. We have rein, leg, and body cues in the one maneuver, the rollback.

Most colts (I say colt but also mean filly) learn faster and better when the rider overemphasizes the weight cues. If we overdo them almost to the point of looking ridiculous, we may get horse laughs from spectators, but we'll also get better work from the young horse.

Years ago I'd often show off when riding a colt for a prospective buyer. I'd hold the hackamore reins in my teeth and work the colt. Almost always the colt would work better than he had the day before when we had no spectators and I held the reins in my hands. At first I thought I was lucky, but then, since this happened to me so often, I asked myself why.

When I held the reins in my teeth, I had to lean way back, as far as I could, to tighten the reins enough to stop the colt. Heck, I wouldn't even get them snug before the colt would start sliding. Though I was nearly keeping the arch out of his back by lying back so far on him, he responded by sliding.

Though such colts knew nothing about neck-reining, they'd turn sharply when I leaned way over so that there'd be rein pressure on their necks. Why?

It slowly dawned on me that my riding position, my ex-

Ken holds the reins in his teeth while stopping a good colt. He's gripping hard and is starting to settle down in the seat.

cessive position changes, were causing this fine work. Riding in this fashion is hard work, much harder than riding straight up, but it works.

The time to do all this stuff is when the colt's green. A green colt, still leery of man, seeks to respond.

When I was manager-trainer at Meridian Meadows, an Arizona man and his family visited us. Right away he started

56

Ken stopping the colt in the normal way.

telling me how everything he saw was wrong. The barn wasn't right. The stalls weren't right. My gear was all wrong.

I didn't say much, but I was getting burned up. Saddling a stud colt that I'd been riding for a couple weeks, I mounted and rode into the arena.

The colt, Baron, worked beautifully, but my critic didn't think so. He was jabbering away at me constantly. When I

57

The author using leg and body aids to stop a filly.

reached the boiling point, I leaned forward, pulled the hacka-more off Baron, and threw it at the man's feet. I folded my arms across my chest and worked the colt at slides, roll-backs and spins. When I looked up, the critic and his tribe had gone.

Now, I grant you, most colts won't work too well under such pressure with nothing on their heads, but it shows what's possible if you eliminate one aid—the rein—and use the other two—legs and weight shifts.

Ken working with Baron with nothing on the colt's head.

So far the colt has been ridden with outside leg pressure, but he doesn't always take the correct lead when asked to lope in circles away from the fence. When you're turning the colt on the fence, the fence is actually another aid, for it stops the colt. Sometimes we're in for a great surprise if we try to do this stuff *away* from the fence. We find that the colt won't work at all.

Sad to say, a colt just may not have the makings of a hackamore colt or, more likely, we just aren't hackamore

59

reinsmen. In moments of panic we've tried doubling from a tight rein, or messing up in so many other ways that the colt is hackamore sour. It takes many years and many mistakes to become a hackamore reinsman. Let's go to the bit.

## COLT BITS

One of my prime inventions is my colt bit guard. I'll make one and illustrate how to do it. We make and sell them, but I'm not picky. Make your own, or have a shop make one

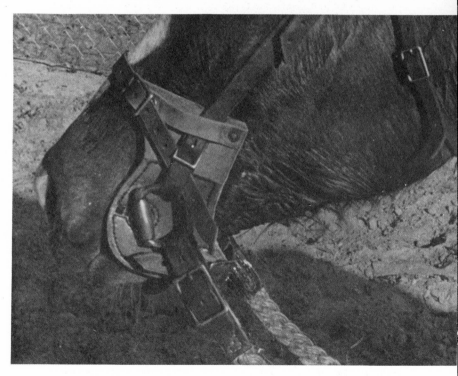

Dave Jones bit guard on a colt.

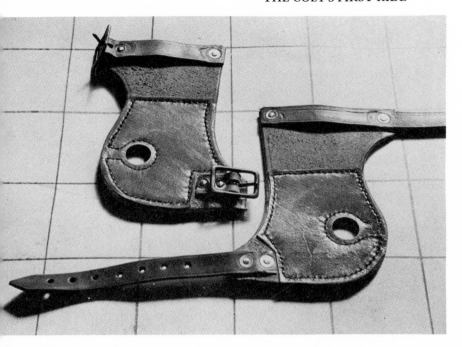

Both sides of a new bit guard. It is laid out on three-inch squares to show the size. The leather and rawhide will be cut in front so that the bit can be slipped in and sewn in place.

for you. Just remember who it was that told you how to do it.

This guard can be set to raise the bit high toward the roof of the mouth by snugging up the nose strap. The colt can't get his tongue over the bit when the bit is in this position. The bit can be lowered as the colt learns how to carry it.

This guard can be set to hinder or allow full action of a snaffle bit (broken bit—jointed in the center). If the colt is very stiff, or unyielding, draw reins might be used. An unguarded bit could be pulled completely through the mouth. The bit guard totally protects the colt's mouth.

There are many varieties of snaffle bits. In California such bits, when used on a western colt, were always used with a running martingale or draw reins, or I should say, this is what I observed. Of course, you don't use such gimmicks in the show ring.

I have to write from personal experience. Personally, I never did have much luck bitting a colt with a snaffle. Mark Smith, an old-time California trainer, once said, "The hackamore is the tool of the rough-handed buffoon while the snaffle bit is the tool of the true horse trainer who has a little finesse about him." Well, he called the tune with me, I guess, for I'm much better with the hackamore than I am with the snaffle bit.

When I'd bit a colt with a snaffle and then put him in a western Pelham (double-rein bit), I'd immediately get much better work out of him. It gradually dawned on me that I'd speed things up somewhat if I just eliminated the snaffle bit.

About 1972 or thereabouts Renalde, Crockett, and Kelly Bit and Spur Company asked me to design some bits for them. I designed the snaffle with alternating steel and copper rollers and a western Pelham No. 62. This Pelham is a good one except that they machine the rollers too perfectly. They'd be better if they were larger and sloppier, although they'd have less sales appeal.

Various writers and trainers dislike Pelhams. John Richard Young is a friend of mine, and we fuss with each other about such stuff. J. R. likes the snaffle bit and full bridle (Weymouth, with double bits). I tell him, "Heck, John, I agree about the double bridle, but you're not going to get many western riders to use them."

J. R. once wrote an article about bits and said the only good Pelham was the S-M polo bit. I dropped him a note

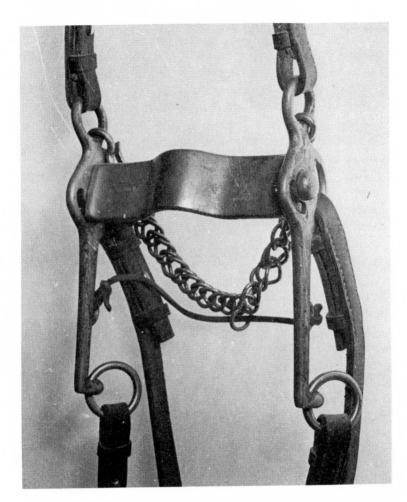

The S-M Polo bit.

saying I agreed that the S-M polo bit was good but that it was notorious for pinching. I also told him that I had a way to rework that bit so it wouldn't pinch.

When J. R. got my letter, he scoffed at it. He'd used the S-M for many years and never pinched a horse with it. That very afternoon he pinched one. He sent me his bit and a letter saying, "You rascal. You must have hexed me."

There's a great variety of English Pelham bits available. The pinching comes about because the head stall ring is so small. When the leverage (bottom rein) is used, the curb chain pinches the corners of the mouth against the mouthpiece. The curb chain needs to be set farther back. Please remember this while I continue.

A Pelham makes a good colt bit if you just remove the bottom rein. Fasten the curb chain snugly, and you won't pull the bit through the mouth.

You can go a few steps farther and make a colt bit from a Pelham. This gives you a mullen-mouth colt bit that isn't broken (hinged) in the center. Since the gentle curve of the mullen mouth follows the contour of the colt's mouth and tongue, we could hardly find a more gentle bit.

If we cut the headstall ring and curb from the Pelham, we have a colt bit. We can go still further and affix copper rollers to the mouthpiece. Colts enjoy playing with the rollers. Copper makes the colt salivate, which helps keep him light.

I buy half-inch copper tubing at the hardware store. I cut five pieces per mouthpiece and cut them two and one-eighth inches long. You can cut them two inches or even shorter if you want the rollers to have a closer fit. I flatten these pieces on an anvil. Then I catch the lip of each piece in a vise and start to bend it around a steel bar of appropriate size. I use a five-eighths-inch bar.

When the roller is partly formed, I remove it from the vise and round it around the steel bar on the anvil. I soon

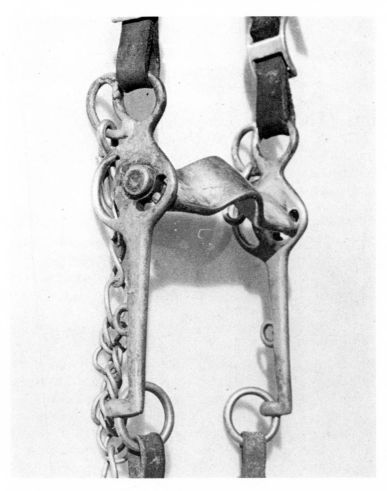

The S-M Polo bit with extra curb-chain provision brazed on.

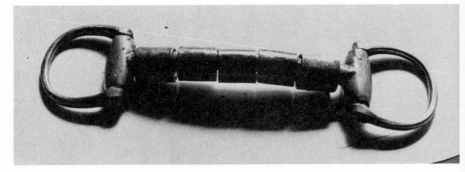

Colt-bit made from an English Pelham.

How a bit guard protects. This filly refused to bend to the right. Her head has been tied around to limber her up.

The filly throws a whingy!

have five round rollers, which I place on the mouthpiece of the bit. I put the rollers, now on the mouthpiece, in the vise and close them up. The final step is to silver-solder the slits closed.

The flux used to get the solder to adhere to the copper should be thoroughly washed off before the bit is used. Of course, you can take the bit and rollers to a machine shop and have a metalworker braze the copper together.

I save all the metal I cut from the colt bits. When I want to add a curb provision to an English Pelham, I have all this "no-rust" hardware at my disposal. I grind the extra rings to fit, hold them in place with small vise-grip pliers, and solder or braze the extra ring into position. This sets the curb chain back far enough that it won't pinch.

She fights so furiously that she finally breaks the headstall of the bridle.

She finally falls. The bridle is broken, but the bit guard is intact, and her mouth is uninjured.

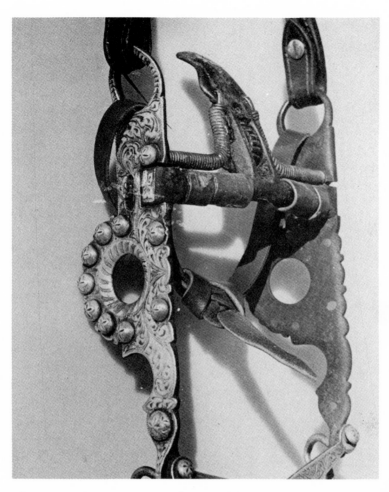

The reworked spade bit. Note slots for the top rein. The mouthpiece
has been bent and rollers affixed.

Many western Pelhams, such as the Monte Foreman, already have an extra slot for a "way-back" curb chain or curb strap. You can add to your supply of bits, however, by reworking Pelhams.

Again, very personally speaking, I see no reason to have a curb bit that can't be used with double reins. To this end I have bored slots in all my old bits to accommodate a top-leverage rein, for the following reasons: (1) safety, (2) out-of-position work, and (3) rider's hand position. As an example of the safety a top-leverage rein provides, one day I was riding a big, stout gelding in the pasture. As we approached my neighbor's barn, a dozen goats jumped up, bleated, and ran around. The startled colt jumped and began to run. I immediately doubled him and got him stopped. Had I tried to double him with the curb part of the bit, he probably would have thrown himself all over me. You should never pull one rein when using a curb bit, for the pain you cause the horse will get you hurt.

The top-leverage rein is also useful for work with "stargazers." Some people brought a mare to me that had never had formal training. She was a terrible stargazer. Her head was always high. She fought martingales and draw reins. Nothing seemed to work.

I had bored holes for top reins on my old spade bits. I had also bent the straight iron mouthpieces of these bits into a mullen-mouth curve. I put a spade on her and gave her some time to get used to it. After a while, I took her for a little pasture ride. I'd removed the bottom rein and was using the spade for a colt bit. Her head position was perfect, and she seemed to enjoy herself.

The angle of the spade makes it mildly uncomfortable for a horse to carry his head too high. Before long, he'll search for a more comfortable position.

With another bit the mare reverted to her old habit of

This horse is in the spade and small bosal—four reins.

stargazing. In the limited time we had to work her, we couldn't get her bitted in anything but the spade.

Let me add a little about the spade bit. It usually takes quite a while to mouth a horse. He's in the little bosal and just learns to carry the spade. Then he's in four reins: the bosal reins and the spade reins. Finally, he's "straight up in the bridle."

The spade bit is fairly heavy. The mouthpiece is always a straight bar. He can't relax his jaw for long, for the heavy

71

bit would lie directly on his tongue. He holds the bit to give himself relief. Then he loosens up and plays with the bit's cricket awhile. On a long ride he has to do this all day, alternating between holding the bit and playing with the rollers.

Years ago I deduced that the straight bar, not the spade itself, was what made mouthing a horse so time-consuming. I heated and bent my bits. Horses bitted right up and enjoyed them. A horse could relax his jaw and let the bit lie over his tongue, for the bit was now curved rather than straight.

I asked a California friend to try my idea. He did so and thought his horses accepted and worked the bit much better.

A word of caution: most bits now have cast rather than iron mouthpieces. If the mouthpiece of your spade bit doesn't rust, don't try to bend it because it will break.

Double reins improve a rider's hand position. When using double reins, the trainer pays more attention to what he's doing. He's not so apt to dope off and slop rein his horse. When he's riding, he's training. Closed reins and romal have the same effect.

A roping rein may be hooked over a rider's finger, and he'll slop his way through a complete training session. Same thing goes for long split reins. The rider will use a mile of slack. When he has to rein or stop, his hand will be up by his chin. Before long his horse will stargaze when being reined or stopped. "Low hands, low head. High hands, high head."

# 6. Work away from the Fence: Inside Lead

I was once tricked into judging a big area show. The horses entered had all won a certain number of points from a four-state region. The show was the work-off. I had to judge Arabian and Quarter Horse pleasure classes. In the Quarter Horse classes there were sixty or more horses each. I was allotted fifteen minutes for each class. I had to pick the top horses quickly.

Judging mistakes was first, and I had to be tough. I knocked down wrong leads and horses that walked at a snail's pace. If horses grouped, a few horses would lay back their ears. Out! If a horse kicked at another one, the kicker was out. I was soon down to about twelve horses.

Asking for extra work is fairly uncommon, but it is a judge's prerogative in Quarter Horse shows. I asked each rider to canter a circle, make a slow stop, and canter a circle the other way. In one class only one horse could manage this simple, basic maneuver. And these horses were all winners!

I thought the Arabian pleasure class was nearly impossible to judge. Walk, trot, walk, canter, walk—both ways and line up to be judged. You simply picked the horse that had been brainwashed the least. I judge no more, for such stuff is a farce. No wonder dressage folk smile and turn away.

I talked to a lady who wanted to ride western but was riding in a dressage clinic. She started western but couldn't find any one who would (or could) give her any sort of intelligent instruction. Her western teachers talked in generalities, using quaint words that had no real meaning. To learn anything useful, she had to go the dressage route.

When we have a little control—can stop and turn on the fence—we should investigate work away from the fence. We may try to stop and turn in the center of the arena. Whoops! The colt throws his head up and goes on. We double, double again, and finally get him stopped. We feel bad, and the colt feels bad, for we thought he had better basic training than no response at all.

Go back to your aids. They are rein, weight shift, leg, and *fence.* You've removed one aid, so you shouldn't be all that upset. The fence gave him a *reason* to stop. When we asked him to stop in the center of the large arena or pasture, there was no reason, so he had to be doubled. Slow down. He has to be taught to work with one fewer aid.

Or we can substitute aids. A cow is as good or better than a fence. The cow gives him a reason to stop. Almost all colts and horses will *immediately* work better if they're asked to work cattle. We want top work rather than *immediate better* work, however, so let's do it right.

We start the colt on cattle just as we would start one destined to be a cow horse—one cow at a time—in a small pen or lane. And please don't use wild cattle. You want the colt to control the cow.

We'll follow the cow until she walks. Then we'll trot around her and turn her back on the fence. When she moves the other way, we'll again trot around her and turn her back. Before long the colt will see that he's turning the cow—controlling her movements—and will enjoy the work.

We can progress daily with this until we're loping past a wilder cow to turn her back. Notice how lightly the colt stops. Notice how quickly he rolls back. He obeys the slightest signal. Voila! See how well he works when we use that substitute aid, the cow.

Pal, a Quarter Horse gelding, is started on cattle. He was so-so when working dry. Pal, a rugged colt, could go any way at this stage of training: reining, roping, or cutting.

Remember, our work fell off out in the arena. OK, we'll work there, but let's go back to the gentle cow. We drive the cow down the arena and rein out around her to the certain place where we control her movements. We'll drive her this way and that, make her circle, and so forth. This is fairly easy with a gentle cow. We want to walk and trot the colt when doing this and never go so far as to get him tired.

75

Pal easily takes a cow off the fence. After a short time Pal found that he could master a calf, and he enjoyed it.

Before long—a week later, perhaps—we can ride fairly close and move out ahead of the cow to block her. We do this at a walk or slow trot. The colt may not stop too well the first few times. Patience! The cow turns the other way. We follow, get out ahead and block again. Pet the colt. Praise him.

Going on with this, we practice daily in the big arena with the gentle cow. Before too long the colt makes some blocks from a very light rein, and we also note that he's stopped and turned a few times before we gave him any signal whatsoever.

If the colt seems to enjoy such work, we may let the last aid, the cow, predominate over the other aids and work toward making a cow horse. If he waits on our other aids, we may try for a reined cow horse. No matter. It's too early to decide.

One might try working a wilder cow in the big arena, but I think that's a mistake. Let's work a quicker cow in a small pen such as a fifty-foot-square bronc pen, or even a wide lane. We want a snappy cow, but we don't want her to have enough room to run much.

When we have the cow contained in the small pen, we can turn her easily. The cow runs, but the colt can trot to head her off just as a top boxer can work his opponent into an ever-shrinking circle. She turns hard and runs the other way. We whirl the colt over his hocks to cut her off again. Wow! We're stopping and turning hard, and we did it away from the fence.

A few hard turns and jump-outs are enough. The colt's using muscles in a way that he hasn't used them before. He could easily become stiff and sore. A devoted human might push himself despite heavy soreness, but it's a sure way to sour a colt. He should be warmed up by long trotting before such work and walked for fifteen minutes to an hour after the work. You can't beat a slow pasture ride at such times.

The colt may be a little clumsy when he's learning to work, so he should be equipped with bell boots, splint boots, and sliding boots. The bell and splint boots protect him from hitting and stepping on himself, while the sliding boots keep him from burning his fetlocks behind. Does a cow horse burn himself by stopping and turning in the arena?

One day I put some new sliding boots on a cow horse,

Way Frey works Syndar, a fine Arabian gelding. The colt is wearing splint boots, bell boots, and sliding boots.

for I was going to do a little roping. Some of the calves made the horse do some pasture blocks as we brought them to the arena. I wanted to see how well the boots stayed in position, so I looked them over before roping. They were slashed and gashed, really torn up from a few minutes' work in the pasture. Common sense tells us that, without boots, the colt will have sore fetlocks after many hard stops and jump-outs.

Depending on how much the colt likes cow work, and on how much we need a cow horse, we may want to rope some

Bell boots over front hooves, splint boots over cannon bones, and sliding boots to protect the rear fetlocks.

cattle before getting into cutting too deeply. We'll go into that in the roping section.

Or we may want to keep on with the cutting. Since each horse is an individual, we have to use common sense in making such decisions. For instance, a man called me about working a filly of his. We went to see her. She was huge but had refinement. He tried to break her each year, but she just kept bucking him off. I took her on.

On her first ride she tried to buck a little, but I discouraged it by yelling and doubling. I roped a log off her on her first ride. She seemed to try to please.

She was so big and stout I thought she'd need a lot of work to keep her contented. So I hauled her over to Arthur Godfrey's Beacon Hill Farm, because there was always plenty

Close-up of bell boots and splint boots.

of cow work there. Her owner couldn't afford to pay for much training.

On her fourth ride I roped calves and dragged them to the crews. I didn't chase the calves. I simply rode into a pen full of calves, dropped a "Hoolihan" loop on one, and pulled him to the crew. This wasn't hard on the filly, and

Close-up of sliding boots.

she really enjoyed it. The rule was, "Miss twice and you're off your horse working with the ground crew." She was so good that I never missed, so I roped at least two hundred calves off her.

For her seventh ride she and I heeled a lot of very wild Brahma cows for blood testing. About a third of the herd crawled out of the six-foot-high chutes. The farm manager headed these wild ones, and I heeled them.

We had opportunities to do some cutting, and she did very well. She was a natural cow horse. After I rode her for a month, the owner made arrangements with the Beacon Hill riders to keep her for free. The owner got back a top horse for almost no training money.

DRY TRAINING: NO COWS

To my way of thinking, there are certain horses—certain strains of horses—that can do things better than others. If you want to train reining horses, you should check out both the individual horse and its bloodlines.

In the 1950s I worked for Charles George Araujo, of Coalinga, California. Charley owned Poco Tivio and leased Doc Bar, bringing the latter into California. When I worked for him, he also owned a sorrel stallion, Jimmie Reed.

Certain horses were in my string. Jimmette, a fine daughter of Jimmie Reed, was one of them. Never before had I ridden such a sliding horse or one who really wanted to slide. I might be riding her to turn back cattle for Charley. She'd make a block, set down, and slide, slide, slide! This was such fun that I'd let her do it, and Charley would yell at me for letting her slide so far she'd go past the cow. "Dammit, Dave, pick her up and stay head to head!"

Later I noted that Jimmette was the dam of Doc's Benito Bar, a sire of reining horses. You can't make a show reining horse if the horse can't slide, and I've ridden many that couldn't.

Any Poco Tivio horse I've ridden could slide well. My horse, Tengo Tivio, stopped and slid any time I asked him to in his working days. His slide wasn't as spectacular as Jimmette's, for he wasn't always looking to slide. He was more cow horse than straight reining horse.

You don't want a cutting or roping prospect to be a natural long-sliding horse. The cutting horse must stop and turn very quickly. If the rope horse slides a long way, he won't stop hard enough to help the roper.

So we don't say that we'll specifically make a contest reining horse unless we have the conformation and breeding to go with it. We might be able to make a fair reining horse

Ken Serco gets down fast. He's teaching the colt to stop on a loose rein. Hand on neck and weight shift are the cues.

out of most, but the ones bred for it will beat us consistently.

Making a reining horse is much easier if we have cattle to work. If we don't we'll have to use a lot of strong cues, and the colt will have to pay attention to them. We used the fence to help the colt stop and turn around, but found that we couldn't do much away from the fence. We lost an aid, so we'll have to strengthen the ones we have left.

Let's walk the colt down the arena, stand up, squeeze hard with both legs, and step down. Before long the colt will associate the squeeze with the stop. He'll shoot his hind legs up under his belly. His rear will drop. Don't do this all the time if you want him to continue doing it, for the novelty of the hard squeeze will wear off rather than develop.

When the colt does this well at a walk, try it from the trot and, eventually, the canter. He should wear sliding boots during his work. If he's the willing kind, he'll improve steadily. He knows how to stop from a lope if we get down. Do everything the same way, but don't get clear down. Now you have a little gimmick to help you: the body shift you make when you get down.

To stop the colt, you might trot him until he breaks into a lope, quickly give him the rein signal, the forward weight shift, the hard squeeze, and the weight shift. When training for the stop, never run the colt a long way before stopping. A few strides at the lope is enough. Be satisfied to stop hard a couple of times in each session. If you overdo the stop, you'll lose it and need cattle to get it back.

For instance, I need a good stop photo. We have a colt in training that slides well. When an apprentice saddles the colt, I mention that I want to take some sliding shots. I go to the office to get a camera. Then I have to load the film. In the meantime the rider tries the colt to check his slide. "Wow, a great slide. Let's try again. Not so good. Next time'll be better. Nope, its worse." When I go out to take the photo, the colt would rather run away than stop.

A good stop in one motion (rather than a series of skips) can be practiced from a circle. Canter a wide circle and draw it down tightly. Let the colt trot when the spirals really get tight. Stop. The colt, while circling, is semicollected and *ready* to stop. After stopping, spin or back the colt.

Never stop and then ride straight forward as the next move. Spin, roll back, or back up after stopping. The colt sees no reason to stop if you simply stop and then go forward. This may seem like nit-picking, but it actually means a great deal to keep work correct.

Most horses are stiff on one side and limber on the other. We could use such popular terms as "hollow," but I'd rather use terminology that's unmistakable in meaning. "Stiff" means "unyielding." "Limber" means "yields too much."

A horse should bend toward the inside, or, if he's cantering a left circle, he should bend to left. If he doesn't bend, he'll lean way over on his side. He can easily slip and fall if he's banked way over.

But here's the problem. Few horses naturally bend toward the direction of the circle. Notice a horse running free in the pasture. When he runs to the right, his head will be cocked way over to the left.

If we train a horse and allow him to work in a very natural manner, the neck rein will emphasize this and bend him completely out of shape. Though the finished product might work a little out of position, he'll be *nearly* straight. You can't keep a horse shaped correctly if you neck-rain him—unless you know how to cheat the neck reins, i.e., pull one rein directly as you lay the other on his neck. The top reining horsemen know how to do this, and they are so slick you can't catch them at it.

Horses are individuals. Sometimes it's nearly impossible to bend a colt "correctly" and have him keep the correct lead. As soon as you bend him to the inside, he drops his lead behind. What is correct? If he's straight, not bent, as he circles—or even a bit off or bent away from the circle— it may be correct for that particular horse. Does this make sense?

Curly was throwing riders by pulling them off. When someone tried to ride him, Curly would root his nose down hard to escape the bit. The rider would hang onto the reins and be pulled forward and off.

Curly tried this with me. I just let the reins slip and allowed him to go on as he pleased. He cantered around with his nose in the dirt for a few minutes and then gave it up. No problem.

I noticed that Curly was very responsive, so I went ahead with him. In a few days, he could actually do a full pass (move directly sideways) at a canter. There seemed to be no limit to what he could do, except he couldn't work when bent correctly. Let him work a little out of position and there was no limit to his good work.

When loping down the arena, he'd come apart if I didn't let him lope bent a little away from whatever lead he was in. He'd slide if I left him in this canted-away position. You're all right with such a horse until you get to the neck-rein stage. Then you have to watch it or your indirect rein will pull him so far out of position he can't work at all.

Back to stiff and limber. A colt will resist on his stiff side. You try to canter a circle. He sets his neck and pulls himself away from the direction you ask him to go. He drifts sideways and is stopped only by the fence. You work him the other direction. His neck bends too much to the pull of the reins. You pull his neck around to your knee, but he keeps right on going straight ahead. Oh, boy. He's a dilly!

There are several ways to limber up the stiff side. The English folk use surcingle and side reins for this. Set the side rein on his stiff side shorter than the other and longe him.

Westerners will "limber him up" by tying his head to his tail, or to the back of the saddle. When I do this, I use a bit guard so the colt's mouth won't be injured. I tie a metal ring to the saddle strings at the base of the cantle and tie the rein to this. A draw rein fastened to the cinch ring and pulled through the bit ring to the ring on the saddle also works well.

I don't believe in leaving a colt tied up too long, nor do I tie him really short. I want him tied short enough that he'll be well bent. He'll test the bit and then accept it. I'll then shorten the rein enough that he'll have to circle, rather than amble about the pen, with his head bent in a little. He may fight it, but will soon stand. Then I'll make him move a little. When he circles without fighting, I say "enough" for I don't want him getting sore.

I now know that he'll accept having his head pulled around without flipping on me. If I hadn't checked him out first, he might have fought me if I pulled him from the saddle, going up and over on me. A little of that goes a long way.

Actually, if he toughens up on me as I ride him, I'm as well off to dismount and tie his head around. If he's fighting the rein, he's doing it to himself, for I'm standing on the ground watching. There's no reason for me to fight him about this.

The limber side is often more of a problem than the stiff side. What do you do when the colt just bends his neck and goes straight ahead?

You must force his body to follow his head. I like a doubled latigo (popper) for this. It makes a noise but doesn't sting. You can use an English crop. You can use a scat bat that steer wrestlers use.

Ride the colt in the bronc pen. Lope him. Make him tighten the circle by popping him on the shoulder or low on the neck. Hit him just hard enough to get the response you want. If you hit him really hard, you're apt to scare him into stampeding with you.

You might turn him with blunt spurs. They even work behind the cinch. I've seen some colts so "sticky" that I'd have to swat them alongside the face with my hat. As soon as they get the idea, you can refine the work by being as gentle as possible. Reward the colt for good work. Don't just hammer on him and cuss him out. You don't get anywhere with colt or child by such treatment. Once you can canter circles *anywhere,* you can move right along with the training.

If we're far enough along on the road to advanced training, we'll start working to make the colt supple. For this I like to use the *inside* leg aid.

Earlier in our training, we slapped the colt on the leg or side of the chest with a stirrup to turn him on a rollback. That was an outside leg aid. He moved from the tap of the boot or stirrup. He moves from the inside leg as well, only he moves the center of his body from the leg.

Think of a hot-dog bun. It's on the table before you. Keep it from moving away with one hand. Press the center of the bun with a finger of the other hand. The center pushes in but the front and back stick out. It's arched away from the finger applying the pressure. This is what happens when you use an inside leg aid.

When the horse is supple, he'll respond to a leg aid used at the cinch or just in back of it. If you use a right leg, his nose will point to the right—a western rider might say that you're bending the colt around your leg. When you're going down the arena with the fence on your left, you'd want the horse to take a right lead, for you're traveling clockwise. Use the right leg. He'll bend to the right as he strikes off into a canter and will take a right lead *if that's his nature.* Remember that some horses have to cant to the left to take and hold a right lead.

You might want to use some exercises especially aimed at making the colt supple. Check your response to the inside leg aid. If you're not getting what you think you should have, use spurs. I'd rather use spurs than kick the colt. Press a spur lightly to the colt. He'll move from it. When you want more response, press harder. *Press,* don't hit him with your spurs.

I use spurs with old silver dollars for rowels. Any good blunt rowel works as well. A sunset rowel with a lot of points isn't rough. A sharp, five-pointed rowel is rough. Of course, whether a spur is mild or harsh depends upon the user.

I have been in situations where I had to spur a horse hard to save both our necks. If a colt is stampeding with you and has set his neck against your pull, you might have to spur hard to break his concentration. You can do this with a blunt spur as well as a sharp spur and not cut the colt.

# 7. Developing Correct Leads

IT'S nice to have horses that are always on the correct lead. Some horses are so naturally handy that they just never take an incorrect lead. Most aren't, and the trainer who works for the general public will have plenty of lead problems handed him.

The horse that's rigid on one side will usually not want to take that lead. He should be put into the bad lead and worked at it until he's ambidextrous—will take one lead as easily as the other. When doing a figure eight, always start on the hard-to-get lead.

Some horses are almost impossible. I once had to train a stallion—an eight-year-old, that had never been on a right lead. I'd sit on him nearly sideways in a position to whirl him into the fence. I'd turn him in, spur on the right side to flex him a little, and whap him over the rump to jump him out *fast.* All this would force him into the right lead, and I'd keep him going until we'd loped around the arena a half-dozen times on the correct lead. After that we'd go for a pasture ride. I couldn't work him too much, for I knew he'd get sore. After a month of this, he'd readily take his right lead. At this writing, we have a huge, eighteen-hand dressage horse here. We're working on two problems. He bucks *hard,* and he won't take his right lead.

We'd been using a semi-Quarter Horse saddle on this horse. After a ride on a hot day, I noticed that he had a foot-long dry spot running vertically down his left shoulder blade. We'd been using a Kodel polyester pad, which really makes horses sweat.

We tried him right away in a full Quarter Horse saddle and noticed that we had no dry spots. Horses don't have to be symmetrical. This horse's left shoulder blade is broader than his right. The saddle interfered with free shoulder-blade movement and caused him pain, so he'd buck and run when asked to canter to the right.

Soon the horse would freely take a right lead. Then he refused. He'd act panicked and run wide. But I had *seen* him freely take a right lead. I knew there had to be more to it than the width of the saddle.

I was giving my wife's old horse some minerals for arthritis and decided to try them on the dressage horse. In a couple of days he freely took the right lead. His appearance changed. His work became light and airy. His ears were forward. When working an extended trot going clockwise, he changed into a canter and took the right lead on the *straightaway.* More about this later in the section on problem horses.

You'll see riders in pleasure-horse classes stop their horses, turn into the fence, and then turn them out when a canter is called. This allows the horse to pivot about forty-five degrees and makes the correct lead much more positive. This is a good way to teach leads. You should cue your horse with inside or outside leg pressure, however, so he'll change on the straightaway. Use whatever works best for you and your horse. Enforce the leg with the spur if necessary.

Some people free the lead leg by shifting their weight to the outside. This works with some riders and some horses. If I've given my cue and the horse takes the wrong lead, I'll try to keep him cantering and put my weight to the outside to make the wrong lead *uncomfortable* for the horse.

For the most part, I think riding *with* the horse is the

ideal. When we worked the colt, the weight cue would be emphasized by riding way over to one side. Lean left for left lead. Make a big, swift change for right lead. Again, what works with one horse won't work with another. The rider's mind should be more flexible than the horse's mind. Do things his way. You'll train better and faster.

Riding deep into arena corners will bend the horse. You do this at a walk, and it's a fine exercise for keeping the horse supple. As you ride through a corner, use your inside leg at the cinch and your outside leg to impel the horse into a canter. He should strike off on the correct lead.

Another lead exercise is to ride to an arena corner and stop the horse. When you continue, he'll have to make a forty-degree turn. A tricky part of this exercise is that you should maintain the gait you start with. If you start at a slow trot, maintain that exact cadence. Don't canter unless you start at a canter. You may drop down to a trot from a canter before stopping. When you stop, the horse should stand in position rather than fidget around. Your horse must travel straight down the arena rather than doing "quarters-in" (having the head out and rear in toward center). This may sound easy, but it's tough to do it correctly.

A serpentine is a good drill. We'll ride across the arena and line up on a post. Ride at it. Turn and go back across the arena. Go up and down the arena in this fashion, making the turn a couple of post lengths long. If your posts are eight feet apart, your turn would be sixteen feet.

When your horse has learned the serpentine at a trot, try the canter. As you approach the fence, ask for a canter —right turn, right lead. As you near the center of the arena, tuck down to a trot. As you near the fence, canter the horse—left turn, left lead. When he becomes ultraproficient, canter the whole thing, changing leads when you're riding straight forward in the center of the arena.

Circling at a canter. The author on Nan's Wimpy Dude. The squaw rein is being used.

Circling is a fine exercise. Remember, I like to vary the circle's size. When it's small, allow the horse to trot to tighten it more; then stop and spin. On a fully trained horse, you can pass up the trotting part: just circle, stop and spin. This makes a fine exhibition when done to music. By the way, music helps. Horses will pick up the tempo and work in time to music. Irish jigs are very good for this.

## THE HALF PASS AND THE FULL PASS

Two-track work is excellent for the western horse. More and more western trainers are using two-track, but sometimes they don't know what they're doing.

A western trainer may start a colt on two-track by pushing sideways on the ground. Technically, this would be the full pass, and it's the last thing you want your horse to learn, not the first.

And they'll put a horse's nose to the fence and spur him to make him move sideways. This is very crude stuff and can easily spoil a horse. I may not start one exactly as a dressage master would, but I work the same way and use the same methods, though the tools are different.

Two-track work is the half or full pass. The tracks the horse's hind legs make don't cover the front tracks—hence, the name. The half pass happens when the horse travels at or less than a forty-five-degree angle. If he's going down the fence or wall, the front legs will be a foot or so more toward the center of the arena than are his hind legs. When he starts, any little distance he travels on two-track is all right. When the horse moves sideways at walk and trot, he's doing a full pass.

Why do them? A trail horse must perform all sorts of intricate maneuvers in today's shows. A pleasure horse should travel straight, but he may naturally travel with his fanny in toward the arena. By being able to control the *whole horse,* we can straighten out the horse that travels crookedly. We can side-pass up to gates. We can work out of tight conditions, such as getting crowded in the ring. I could go on and on, but you get the idea.

Here's how I start. Most arenas have a well-worn path near the rail or fence. The horse is used to traveling this path and wants to be in it. I'll ride him parallel to the track.

Holding his head straight ahead, I'll use intermittent leg pressure to push him over to the track. In a very short time, he'll be moving in that direction. I'll keep this up until it's automatic. Before long I can be twenty feet from the track and two-track him over to it. Usually, one side is easy, while the other side is harder to get. As with any other exercise, I'll work the toughest side most until I consider him working both sides equally well.

Going further, I can soon work him back and forth across the arena on two-track. I'm sure you've seen movies of riders doing this as an intricate drill at the Spanish Riding School. This is part of their daily work.

Before long I'll ride straight ahead on the track near the rail. I'll bring the horse's head and shoulders out toward the center of the arena, while his hind legs stay in the track. This is the half pass and it's called "shoulders in." The reins hold the colt in, while the leg forces the shoulders out. If he weren't held in (collection), he'd simply walk out in the arena in response to the leg aid. A few steps are enough. If you feel that he might stop (lack of propulsion), let him straighten out immediately. Have him moving forward freely before asking for the two-track again. You don't want him getting sticky and stopping whenever he wants to. That's why working the nose to the fence (quarters in) is a poor drill. It teaches him that he can stop when he wants to or work in a jerky, spastic fashion.

At first the steps he takes doing shoulders in will be crude and rough. No matter. Practice will refine it. He'll respond to a lighter rein and a lighter leg signal after he learns what he's doing. Take your time. Let him learn this easily so he'll enjoy it. Let him think it's his idea. Praise him for good work. Do not haul back harshly or spur with force. Be nice. Be gentle.

The full pass, wherein the horse travels sideways, is simply a more collected version of the half pass. The farther along he goes, the more acute is the angle he'll work, until he works sideways or *nearly so.* You must pay particular attention to see that the shoulders lead the quarters, that his front end is always slightly ahead of his rear end. Get them reversed and the horse will stick, stop, learn to work out of position, and lose his propulsion.

When you work across the arena—full pass to the right—the shoulders will lead the quarters, but the neck and head will be slightly bent to the left in response to the left leg. At first this bend will be very noticeable, but you'll work to get the horse straighter as time goes by.

When you approach the fence, you'll want to reverse the aids to work to the left. There will be a slight pause. Your aids will move the horse's shoulder to the left so that it leads the quarters. You make sure that the horse starts out with shoulders leading the quarters.

Early in this training you'll probably need two dressage whips. Buy the longest ones you can find. Get the stiffest ones available, for they're very "whippy." You might even start out with two tree branches about forty-two inches long, long enough to reach the horse's quarters. You don't want to change your hand position on the reins while using them, so they need to be quite long.

I believe that it's very important for the horse to have no fear of the whips. Go over him with them by quietly rubbing them over his body. Before long you should be able to swish a whip over his head while he stands calmly. The rope horse learns to stand as the rope's whirled over his head. It should be the same with whips.

The whip is another aid, an extension of your arm. You can use it to alert the horse, move him better in two-track, help him change leads during the figure eight, and, flicked on the forelegs, will help in backing the horse fast and straight.

So let's talk about the figure eight. There are a couple of ways to teach a colt to do a proper figure eight. First, you might have a catty horse that will switch naturally, and you have no problem. Horses bred for cutting, the small, strong, catty ones, will be naturals.

But let's say we're working a Thoroughbred-type Quarter Horse. He's been a bit clumsy but has learned, through long hours and wet saddle blankets, to work well. He'll take either lead readily, and that's what we need.

Lope a circle. Stop. Lope a circle the other way. We've done a lot of this. We've loped a circle, tucked down to a trot, and loped the other way. No problem. Let's make a long, teardrop-shaped circlet. When we're on the straightaway, after the first circle, we'll reverse cues and strike off in the other direction. With some speed he should change. Going slower, he may change in front but not behind. Let's use the dressage whips.

Let's ride a circle at a canter. When the circle is completed, let the horse straighten out for a couple of strides, and then signal for a lead change. In addition to the other cues, flick the horse's quarter with the dressage whip. At first this may startle him. With a little practice you'll find that the lightly used whip will help him change front and back together.

Speed will help the horse perform the flying change without whips. The whips will help at a canter. When the horse can automatically change leads correctly at a canter, you can vary the speed. Don't subject the horse to much of this in a single day, for it's mentally tiring.

The horse breathes through the nostrils, not the mouth. Most Arabian horses have large, flaring nostrils that allow them to breathe freer and work longer than other breeds. Don't ask your horse to drill, drill, drill without allowing him time to regain his breath. This is one reason to put the corner stops in your drills. It allows the trainee time to regain calm breathing.

Likewise, a horse usually becomes an unthinking animal when he's hot. When working on hot, humid days, such as we have here in Florida, limit your work and pay attention to your horse's condition. He can think when he's cool.

Deep in the Colombian tropics the weather is so hot and humid that horses can't be used for working cattle. Horses will continue to work when they are overheated and will die. Mules are used instead. When a mule becomes hot, he stops.

When managing a Paso farm in Tallahassee, we'd often have to catch a big yearling or two-year-old and break him to lead during the hottest part of the day. He'd be very hot before we even caught him.

He'd be run into a chute, blindfolded, and haltered. A long, soft rope would be passed through the halter and tied around his neck with a bowline knot. The blindfold would then be removed and the chute gate opened. The colt would charge into the breaking pen. Whoever had the rope would try to make it to the snubbing post. The rest of us would haze the colt toward the post. When he was snubbed short, the rope would be tied off, and we'd retire to give him a little time to realize that pulling back didn't mean escape. Soon we could approach him, and he wouldn't set back on the rope.

If the weather was reasonably cool, we'd gentle him right there. We'd handle his hooves and break him to lead. But if the weather was hot and humid, we'd untie the rope and half-lead and then half-haze him to get him to the covered arena out of the sun. Once there, he'd be hosed down with cool water. When his body temperature had returned to near normal, we could go ahead and gentle him. Without being cooled off, he'd fight until he dropped.

## THE SPIN

The spin, like the slide, is best performed by horses that have proper conformation. If a horse is strong behind with legs neither too crooked nor too straight, he should be able to spin. What has always surprised me is the number of horses that can spin even without the asset of top conformation.

There are several ways to teach a colt to spin. Ed Connell explained two methods in his fine book *Hackamore Reinsman.* The colt learns the set and turn, or rollback. When he does this effortlessly, he's turned away from the fence and jumped out, making a complete revolution plus jump-out. Then he performs a circle and a half, always finishing with the jump-out that keeps the speed in the spin. Ed's other method, and a longtime favorite of mine, is to have the horse canter a diminishing circle until asked for a stop and a spin. I've used both methods, and they're fine work for the hackamore colt.

The modern method is also one I've used for many years, and it's much like teaching the dressage pirouette. The modern aspect of it is that today's trainers want it low, flat and fast. To keep it low, I favor a low-set running martingale. Walk the colt in a circle that gets smaller. When the circle is very tight, lie back on the horse and pull and release the reins to hold him in position (from moving forward). Bump him around with boot heel, spur, bat, or dressage whip. As with everything else, one side will be somewhat sticky.

By leaning way back and bumping the bit, rather than pulling and using an aid to rotate the front of the colt, we start getting that low flat spin. Don't rush. He'll cross one front leg over the other rather than skip around, and he needs time to learn how to place his legs before trying any

The filly Ken Serco is riding is somewhat ewe-necked. He is using the snaffle bit and running martingale. The filly has learned to work with leg and weight-shift aids. Ken rides her without using the reins.

fast spins. If you work ahead of your colt and yourself (just to see how fast he can spin), he'll walk all over himself, get sore, dread work, and give you a problem to solve.

At a clinic put on by an Ohio reining expert, I showed how working the set and turn off at a fence could lead to the start of the spin. The reinsman didn't like this way of doing things and said so to the audience. He pointed out the shortcomings of this mode of operation, saying that the colts worked too high and couldn't turn fast enough. I was show-

Ken is asking the filly to spin. Note that one leg is crossing over the other. She has a long way to go, for her conformation doesn't favor a low head.

ing the antique spin rather than the hot, low, and fast modern spin.

But the day before I had worked with the reinsman's top rider. After a little "antique" work, the young man told me that a couple of colts worked much better in ten minutes than they had in two months with "modern" methods.

101

Relicario with the author up, starting a spin to the right. The horse spins very fast. He's already throwing dirt from his planted hind hooves. He is ready to swing his left foot around. The weight is leaving his right front leg.

Using the old way, I've made spinning horses that could spin so fast you'd be terribly dizzy after going around six times. I've ridden such horses that "old-timers" have made, and they'll spin so fast it'll scare you.

Some rules call for spins to end with jump-outs, long arena runs, and spins the other direction. There is a forward propulsion to such work. The modern method often lacks forward propulsion. When the rider relaxes, the horse "dies." This is why a couple of horses worked better after rolling back and jumping out at the reinsman's clinic. We kept the forward drive and speed in the half circle, which led to keeping speed and drive in the spin. The horses kept their hind legs still rather than walk around on them, using the front legs to propel themselves around in the circle.

The dressage pirouette is taught much like the modern flat spin, except that the horse is up in the bridle and forward impulsion is never lost. It's not a low, hot, flat spin. The dressage trainer considers it one of the most difficult things to teach because (1) he continually watches out for loss of propulsion, and (2) the dressage horse isn't as apt to have the conformation for it.

In all training, the trainers look for different things in their horses. The cutting-horse man would be helpless if he had to make cutting horses out of, say, Hanoverian or American Saddlebreds. The dressage rider would quit after a few days of trying to make dressage horses out of Tennessee Walkers. When a trainer offers instruction, he must use the type of horse that fits the kind of training he does. He must also understand conformation. A horse can't slide if his hind legs are straight as a ruler. A horse that's weak behind and heavy up front can't rein. A good, balanced conformation that fits the horse's breed is what one looks for.

# 8. The Neck Rein and the Finishing Bit

WHEN the colt is put into the finishing (curb) bit, he should be neck-reining well if he's supposed to neck-rein. "Whoa," you say. "We're neck-reining and bitting the horse? Jones, you haven't said anything about neck-reining."

Well, I have, in a way. When I talked about overemphasizing body-shift cues, I mentioned holding the reins in my teeth and working with nothing on the colt's head. That, friends, is ultrareining.

When your colt responds to the various aids, you simply substitute the indirect rein for the direct rein. In a few minutes he'll be doing a fine job, if you're using all the other aids.

Way back in the colt's training period, however, we had to use one hand to control the horse when we reached to open a gate or roped off the colt. At such times we pulled one rein. The other rein hit the colt in the neck. We were using the squaw rein, even if we didn't think about it as such.

When I squaw-rein, I like to get as many fingers as possible between the reins. One rein will be held out with my "pinkie," while the forefinger pushes the other out. At more hectic times, I'll simply have the reins coming in and running out different sides of my fist. This is difficult when you're roping, but proficiency makes it easier. The squaw rein is an intermediate step between the low wide rein and the neck rein. Taking in the reins—using a side pull and release—but not in a low wide fashion—is the second step: (1) low

Low wide rein. The right hand holds the mecate at the center. The left hand moves down and takes the rein.

Squaw rein.

wide, (2) reins are pulled from each side of the saddle horn, (3) squaw-rein, (4) neck-rein.

When the hackamore is used, the trainer should search for the one the colt works best in. We have (1) thick-stiff, (2) thick-limber, (3) medium-stiff, (4) medium-limber, (5) light-stiff, and (6) light-limber hackamores. The limber hackamores or bosals are easier on the colt. The stiff ones make it easier to double him.

When we get down to the thin-under-the-bridle bosal, this noseband is a half inch or less in diameter. The *chicita* bosal, or *bosalito,* is pencil-sized and goes under the bridle as a permanent fixture, except at shows.

A thin mecate is used with the light, four-rein bosal. Traditionally, the colt is ridden in the four-rein bosal and just carries the bit for some months. Then the reins are attached and used a little until the vaquero, *amansador,* or jinete thinks the *potro* works in such fine fashion that he can go straight up in the bridle. He will be neck-reined during the four-rein stage, and is always neck-reined in the bridle. The reins are held in one hand, no fingers between the reins. They enter at the heel of the hand and come out between thumb and forefinger. A romal is usually used with these reins, which are always closed (as opposed to open or split).

The split-rein reinsmen hold the reins as one would hold a hose when watering the garden. From bit to rider's hand, they enter and are held by thumb and forefingers, or thumb and second finger, for it's permissible to have a finger between the reins. When holding the reins in this fashion, it's possible to use a squaw-rein version, pulling and neck-reining at the same time.

The big problem with any kind of reining is going from long, slack rein to short, collected rein. When actually reining, the reins have to be held short enough that the rein hand is down and right over the horn, rather than up under the rider's chin.

The ultraloose-rein rider apes the cutting-horse man who rides with his reins very long to show the judges that he's not reining his horse. He speaks of "bumping" rather than reining and uses a heavy rein to bump with. He'll bump (let the rein bump the neck) his horse to show him what cow he wants to separate.

This long, "slop" rein looks neat and is copied. When the rider wants to stop his horse from such a loose rein, however, he'll have to pull over his head to tighten the reins.

If a horse is neck-reined from a slop rein, the indirect rein will be tight, while the other will just flop around. This pulls the horse's head away from the direction he's supposed to be going. Both reins should be as low and even as possible when neck-reining.

The neck rein, unless practiced by the reinsman, will spoil a horse. When the reins are held in the correct position, you lose a lot of their normal give and take.

As I said before, my bits are reworked to allow double-rein use. If a bridle horse starts to mess up, he can be corrected if the bit allows direct-rein use.

Steel Helmet was working well straight up in the bridle for the most part. His stops and spins were very good. His figure eights were perfect. But if I wanted to roll him back on the fence, he'd cheat me. When I'd stop, he'd jump sideways and lie up against the fence rather than roll back. In the curb bit I had no way to correct him. All I had to do to roll him back was to use double reins. After I stopped, I'd pull his head to the fence, roll back, and jump out.

Even the old reliable horse may become frightened and run away from the "monster." You can't double him in the curb bit (or damn well shouldn't).

When I hear the words, "You can't show a horse in double reins," I start getting a headache. You don't train at shows. Ride with your curb rein at a show. If you mess him up a little, go home and straighten him out. By doing so, you'll help all your horses that work off a bit. Cutting horses and rope horses can work the curb bit, since they're self-workers and do not rely 100 percent on the rider's signals.

If you like fine California bits, look at bit catalogs carefully. You'll usually find one or more bits that actually have a slot where the top rein should go on a western Pelham. There's no reason not to buy a bit that's 50 percent more versatile than others.

You who think that three hundred dollars is a little much for a bit can find many fine western Pelhams that can be used two-rein at shows and four-rein at home.

When you use double reins, you'll sit up straighter, use a much better hand position, and be more apt to actually train when you ride. You can use a running martingale on the top rein. Work will improve dramatically.

Don't fall for any of the old, diluted prune juice about crossing reins under the horse's chin to "teach him to neck-rein." Just go ahead and neck-rein him along with your other aids, and he'll work in fine fashion.

# 9. Training the Rope Horse

FIRST things come first, so the first thing with a rope horse is to break him out right. He ought to be going pretty well and reining very well before we go to our first calf. Of course, we have also roped off him a fair bit to accustom him to the whine of the rope, and we have pulled objects up to him, such as blocks of wood, weeds and branches.

OK. Let's start rating calves. If this is to be just a ranch rope horse, this will be the most important thing he can learn.

We'll arm ourselves with a bat and go out to the cattle. Let's pick a calf out of the bunch, preferably a slow one to start with, and follow him around, staying behind him just the distance we like to rope from—our correct rating position. We'll bat the horse up if he is too far behind, and pull him in if he gets too close, until we are staying just where we want to be.

When the calf gets tired, we'll go after another one. Horses like to play with cattle like this, but don't overdo it and tire the colt.

When rating is down pat, rope a calf. Catch a good calf around the neck and gradually stop the horse. If there's a helper, let him remove the rope and stay on the colt.

I like to dally-rope at this stage of the game, especially if I have to work by myself. If something goes wrong, I can drop the rope and not spoil my horse by getting him all tangled up and rope-burned.

Let's say that I am by myself. I follow the calf until he

The author has just caught a calf. This is the first day this gelding, Pal, has been roped from.

starts to tire, then I rope him. I keep the horse going until I ride up close and dally. My horn is wrapped, so I take two dallies, get off, and hold the end of the rope so the dallies won't hop. I also have my horse dallied up close. The calf is a little tired and not too rank to start with, so he doesn't fight me and scare the colt back.

I stick my hand into the loop, and release my hold on the end of the rope. The rope comes off the horn, and I keep hold of the loop, which opens up and releases the calf. If I had been tied on, chances are I would have had to leg down the calf and tie it to get my rope back.

I will now ride the colt around a little to make sure he is gentled down. He has been rewarded for doing a good job on the calf, and we are very friendly with each other. We will

111

The author's hand has hold of the lariat around the calf's neck. He has just released the dallied rope with his right hand, and the rope is hopping off the horn.

now go catch another calf and go through the same thing. Then we call it a day.

I enjoy dally-roping, so I keep doing so quite a while. If the horse's path bends toward the rodeo arena, I will have to start tying the rope to the horn and tying down the calf.

If that's the case, I tie the rope hard and fast, make sure I am packing a sharp knife, and go rope a calf. I equip the horse with a backup rope, so I will be able to keep him from following me up to the calf.

The backup rope is a piece of clothesline that runs from the bit to a pulley on my fork and ends up looped in my

Horse, calf, and roper take a rest.

belt. It is a little longer than the lariat. This backs up the colt after I get off and go to my calf.

Some guys (rough and tough ones) just slap the horse in the face and scare him back. I think the horse should understand his part in helping up-dump the calf, so the backup rope is my way of doing business. The horse soon understands that when I go after a calf, he is to back up and keep that rope tight. If you've ever tried to leg-down or flank a calf with a horse that comes up and gives you a slack rope, you know as well as anyone how important the tight rope is. Keep the backup rope rigged until the horse flies back and

113

Rope play. Just fooling around, heeling a calf.

does it every time. If you have to use your green colt at a contest, use the backup line in the arena. It would be better to keep the colt out of contests as long as possible, since excitement does a lot to foul up the colt. He will be good for a long time if we take plenty of time getting him going.

The roper's box can make or break you. You might have a great rope horse, but if he goes crazy in the box, you're out of luck. He should willingly enter the box, stand there collected, break out fast (when you want him to), run well

"Lookit, Ma, I got 'em both."

to the calf, rate the calf perfectly, stop hard to bust the calf, and work the rope perfectly when you're off and away from him.

The box is often the undoing of us all. To get the horse to go in and stand there when he knows that he will soon come out running as fast as he can is something that takes coolness and brains in both the horse and the roper.

We can start out by getting the horse to like the box. Feed him in it. Groom him in it. Feeding and grooming him in the box will make him want to go into the box.

115

Rewarding Pal for a job well done.

Ride in and out of the box. Ride in, loosen the cinch and air the horse's back there. Do all you can to make him want to go in the box.

Now we want to get the horse to stand in the box without breaking out on his own when the chute bangs open. To do this, let's get him used to the chute banging open. He hears the noise and it's like a starting gun. If the calf freezes in the chute, the horse goes out anyway.

We'll bang that chute open while we feed him, groom him, and air his back. We'll sit on him and bang that chute

116

and still keep him in the box. Soon we'll have him where the chute banging open doesn't bother him too much.

Same way with calves. We'll release some and never go out of the box after them. We'll keep this up for a long time. Rope one, release one, rope two, release one. This is necessary, for if the horse comes right out after the calf, he would break the barrier at shows where the calves are given a long score.

Patience, patience, and more patience! When the horse starts doing something wrong, correct it! It'll take quite a while before we can hit the line just right to shave off the fraction of a second that might give us the winning time. We have to rope many calves before we have a rope horse, and many more before we have a rodeo horse. We may never have one that will put us in the pay line.

We should always pad the rope horse's back pretty heavily, because the calf creates quite a shock when he hits the end of the rope. If the back cinch isn't tight, the saddle will rise up in back and the horse will come up to relieve the pressure on his withers, thus fouling up the calf tier-upper. If the horse drags the calf while the roper is endeavoring to make the tie, loosening the flank cinch should keep the horse from overworking.

There's a lot of controversy about tie-downs. Some folks wouldn't use one anytime, anywhere. I don't think any calf roper feels this way. If his horse needs a tie-down, he puts one on him. It's pretty hard always to hold your reins right with all the speed and excitement of calf roping. We can't blame the roper for this, so when that head starts shooting way up on the stop, put on that tie-down. It's not a question of ethics but dollars. A horse does run freer and work better without a tie-down. The man who really trains his horse to stop without getting off on the reins has the problem pretty well whipped.

Now, some horses just don't seem to want to stop without the rein. Here's how to see if they will. I like to work the very green colt on easy calves—not small, just not too rank. After I have roped quite a few calves and the horse has some idea of stopping after the calf is looped, I slap the horse on the neck to get his attention, then bail off. The horse should then stop and work the rope. The colt will generally catch on pretty fast when he's learning and interested. He'll start stopping better the faster I get down. It's best to get down during the jerk. When we graduate to ranker calves, the whole process should go smoother.

When we hear of nine- and ten-second times in calf roping, we can generally figure that the calves are easy. This is all right once in a while in a contest, but the horse doesn't learn too much from it. Big, rank calves are the thing for good rope work. In the spring, when we want to ready up for the roping year, we may be forced to get little calves. If we do, we'll be disappointed in our rope horse when we get into an arena with rank calves.

Here's the difference. We come out after a little calf and throatlatch him. We bail off, bust the calf, go under the rope, flank the calf down as he's getting up, and throw on the wraps and the "hooey" (two wraps and a half hitch). All the horse has done is stop and back up, which is about all he ever has to do if he really "powders" the calf. But, if we get a bad run, a zigzag calf, or snag a bundle of really rank cowhide, we're in a storm. If we don't get a good "bust" on the calf, he may wrap up the horse in the rope.

We can give the horse a little rope work and play by catching the calf in a place in the arena where the horse can't bust him, or we can acquire a few really rank calves to rope at home. This is a good way for the horse to learn to keep his eye on the calf while working the rope.

In this day of ultrafast roping, many ropers carry only one rope. I always carry two, because sometimes a dollar can be made with the second loop.

I tie this second rope with three wraps of good string around a small D ring tied onto my fork. This rig has not come down for me yet, but, when I want it, the small D cuts the string when I pull.

I use a second loop at home, often on purpose, to keep the horse used to that dragging first rope. When a miss is made with the first loop, I get my leg and fender over it, yank the second loop, and fly after that calf.

When we rope a lot of fast, straightaway calves, the horse may get used to blasting out wide open and refuse to follow a turning calf. If we can't get turning calves to play with, we can always get a few goats. Too much goat-roping spoils the horse, because he will scotch (slow down) waiting for the goat to turn. A little of this is all right, though it depends on the horse. If the horse is prone to scotch, he can't be slowed up much without really spoiling him, but a smart, rank goat will sometimes help the horse and also sharpen up the roper's eye.

I believe all good ropers are patient men. They have to be, or there would be few good rope horses. A rope horse, a really good one, is hard to make, and not all horses can make the grade. Coolness in the box, terrific sprint, hard stop, cow sense, and the agility of a mountain goat are requirements for a rope horse. And *keeping* a horse good requires real savvy.

This spring, a couple of fine fellows brought three mares to breed to my stallion Tengo Tivio. While they were here, each ordered a saddle and asked me for a few pointers about roping. They were soon going to a team-roping school.

I've done a lot of team roping on ranches but none in the arena. It's done the same way, however, so I feel quali-

Above: It takes agility. This calf fell when the author pulled his slack. The horse could have flipped over it but managed to miss it. Very dangerous.

Opposite top: Contest roping. This roper has caught and is turning his hand to jerk up slack. He is using a padded tie-down.

Opposite bottom: Contest roping. The roper has caught and is getting down on the right side. He has pitched the slack up and away so that the horse won't get caught in it. He is using a backup rope.

The horse is holding a tight rope. The roper is pushing the calf's hind legs up in order to make the tie. A piggin' string is on the calf's right front leg. The slack rope hanging from the horse is the backup rope.

fied to write about it. Let's start with the basics. And I want to add that what I say about roping is my idea, not what someone has told me.

Neither of my friends threw what I consider to be a flat round loop. They used a lot of wrist motion, and the loop would start to rotate as it went out. This might catch a calf or cow close up but wouldn't work if you had to reach out very far.

At a small local rodeo, I noticed a friend catch a calf by

the right hind leg. He got down and made a pretty swift tie. Later I said, "Bill, how the heck can you tie a calf so fast with a hind-leg catch?" Bill said, "You could too if that's the only way you ever caught one."

At that time I was roping pretty fair and thought I knew what I was doing. I've seen fellows give me a dirty look and load their horses when I pulled into a rodeo.

A few years later I found myself training rope horses for a Virginia cow outfit. Sometimes I'd rope calves all day.

One day a big colt reared up with me. I thought he was coming on over, so I turned loose and had a long hard fall. I sprained my right wrist.

I wanted to rope while my wrist was still sore but found that it really hurt when I used it. For the heck of it, I splinted and bandaged it so rigidly that it couldn't flex at all. I never roped as well before. I had to use a lot of arm motion and no wrist motion.

My loop went out with no rotation. I could reach way out and still keep a flat open loop—of course this can be varied. When up close, the wrist can be used. I showed this to my friends, and they were amazed at the flat open loop I threw.

If you're roping low-headed calves, you get your arm up as high as possible to give a more downward, acute angle to your throw. To practice this on the ground, I set a hay bale on its side and rope directly behind it. catching only the front end. To make it tougher, rope on a slope with the bale down-slope from you. To make it easier, rope with the bale up the slope.

To practice heeling, rope the back end of a sawhorse. Tie it to a fence so that the back legs are eight or more inches off the ground. The easiest and surest way to heel is to throw a trap loop. The header throws a flat loop and ropes horns. He dallies up as close as possible. He can stop and turn back. This will drag the steer in a straight line. The heeler

123

rides behind and to the left of the steer. His loop hits the back of the steer's legs. The front part of the loop "breaks" and flips around to stand up in front of the steer's legs. The header drags the steer into the loop. Slack is pulled. The heeler dallies, and the ropers have the head and hind legs. This is the slow way, though some contest ropers almost work this way.

The contest header catches horns and veers off hard to his left. This swings the steer in an arc. The heeler slaps a loop down as the steer swings. Timing has to be perfect. Learn the former way, and vary it as you become proficient.

I'm making a lot of saddles that will be used for breaking colts and for team roping. The swells are wider and higher than on the slick calf-roping saddles. The cantle is higher and straighter. A four- or five-inch shovel cantle will keep the header's rope from digging into his leg. Most of these saddles have a heavy rawhide cantle binding so the lariat won't chew it up.

Twenty years ago the silk manila was the best handling rope you could get. Government restrictions on the quality of the fibre were lessened, so the ropes got pretty bad. Some manila and sisal ropes are used today. I'm becoming fond of the superpoly ropes, for they seem pretty usable when they're new. Nylon ropes are getting better. A new nylon rope used to be a terrible thing to break in.

The owner of the Virginia cow outfit where I trained rope horses had a couple of old raggy nylon ropes. I ordered two new ones and hated them. I'd rope a calf, and there'd be this calf's neck-size kink in the rope.

One day Frank, the owner, came around. I smiled "lovingly" at him. He said, "What the hell's wrong with you?"

"Gosh, Frank," I said, "I just like you. I think you're quite a man."

He looked surprised. I went on.

"Frank, I just need to show you how much I like you. I'm gonna trade you my new best-quality-you-can-buy nylon ropes for your ol' raggy ones."

"You will?" he asked, puzzled.

"Sure," I said. And we swapped.

On the way home I stopped at the grocery store and bought a lot of paraffin. When I got home, I melted the paraffin in a can and ran the lariats through it, hand over hand.

Then I heated the oven to 300 degrees, tied the ropes so they wouldn't lap, placed them in a foil-lined cookie pan, and shoved the whole mess in the oven for a half hour.

Later I saddled a horse and had a friend help me. I took a turn of rope around a post, dallied the rope, and had my friend hold the end to keep tension on the rope. This smoothed off the rough paraffin pieces and drove the stuff down into the rope. Before long I had two ropes that looked like new and had more weight to them. They'd sail much better. Frank had a heck of a time with his new ones.

# 10. Choosing and Training the Cutting Horse

MOST admirers of the western stock horse have seen cutting horses work in the arena. Many have ridden cutting horses, and a few have trained them. When you see a horse really duck and dodge while heading a cow, you can bet that horse has much natural ability and has had many hours in the practice arena with a top trainer on board. A cutting horse must enjoy cow work. He also needs practice and experience so he will make the right move at the right time.

The western horse has a lot of heritage as a stock horse, and I believe that the ability to work cattle is somewhat inherited. This is easy to find out about our own horses. If, in the normal course of working cattle, the horse makes a few good moves on his own with his eye on the cow, we have something that can be developed.

There are exceptions to this, of course. A colt may have been spoiled, for instance. If the colt fears of his rider, or has had his mouth yanked and hauled on, he'll have his head up and won't be able to see anything lower than an eagle. Everyday handling and proper breaking also affect the green horse just started. Trainers have different methods. Sometimes one trainer has difficulty settling a colt down, where another trainer might be successful.

A cutting horse must be able to turn fast, with his head low. Pivoting on the hindquarters is essential. A horse that turns on the front end won't be able to hold rank cattle.

A cutting horse takes a terrific pounding through the years, so he should have the bone and back to take it. A horse with poor legs just can't stand the gaff. Good withers are another requisite. No matter how tight you cinch up, if the horse is mutton-withered and round-backed, the saddle will shift when you're cutting cattle. I am not saying that a round-backed, mutton-withered horse will not make a cutting horse, only that he would be a better one with good withers. We want a well-built, intelligent horse that likes to put a cow in her place. If we have such an animal, the battle is half won.

STARTING THE COLT

It seems to me that one thing we especially must avoid is making the colt afraid of his head. Many trainers advocate the snaffle bit, and some colts work best in it. I like the hackamore for most colts, and I'll be as gentle as possible with it.

I sometimes saddle the colt in his stall, put the hackamore on him, and let him do some of his own head positioning. I don't tie the head too tight but allow enough slack so that he can flex his neck, tuck in his chin, and take the pressure off the nose.

The next step is to get the colt going easily, and this means take your time. I generally drive the colt enough to teach him to start, stop, turn, and back, as discussed earlier. I like to ride in a small pen so the colt has no place to go and can't run wide open. Just ride around the pen, and try to get the colt to relax. If you manage to move the colt, turn both ways, get him stopped, and get off, you have made a good first ride. Keep him in the small pen until he is relaxed and will move around with his tail carried freely, not tucked up tight. He should be handling a little and stopping for you to get off before you move up to a larger pen.

To tie mecate reins and lead on the noseband, I use this method, which a trainer friend showed me back in 1949. I've never found a better way. It's simple and puts the reins and lead where you want them. There shouldn't be more than one wrap in front of the reins. Push the end of the mecate between the sides of the hackamore. Take as many wraps as needed, and then pull the reins through as illustrated.

Take one wrap over the reins. Push the reins back in order to form two loops. Run the other end of the mecate through the loops as shown.

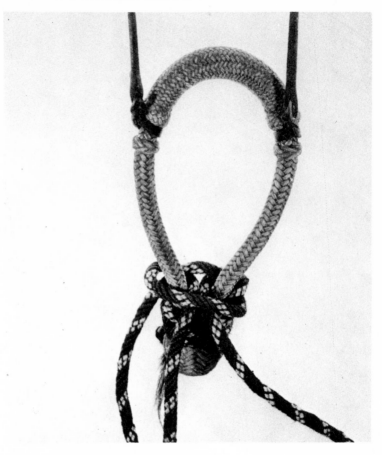

Pull everything snug, and it's ready to use.

Never pull steadily on the hackamore rein. To turn the colt, hold your hand way out so he can see it, and turn him with easy pulls and releases. You are then taking the colt's head. Since he does not know just when you are going to pull him, he cannot prepare for it and set his neck against you. Just one ride using a steady pull will take many rides

130

to correct, so we should allow no one to ride the colt unless the rider has good hands and understands the correct principles of handling the hackamore.

Should the colt want to buck or run, double him. The double is the "brake" when hackamoring a colt. The colt responds to a light pull straight back with one rein, or he gets doubled. He soon respects the double and acts accordingly.


STARTING ON CATTLE

If the colt is going pretty well and is strong, a little association with the cow is in order. General cow work—roundup, herd-holding, penning, and so on—would do him a lot of good. It's my contention that a young horse should learn how to do many things. He should help his rider open gates by sidling up to them, and a little knowledge of the rope is never amiss. General cow work and handiness at an early stage is good for any colt.

So, let's say our prospective cutting horse is handy, switches leads easily, and can stop and roll back all right. We now have a colt ready to start on cattle. Of course, any outline of training is a guide only, since every colt will be different. For instance, one colt might respond to the shifting of body weight and neck-rein so easily and naturally that we always neck-rein him after the first month or two of training. Another colt might go out of position and foul up if we speed him up too much. But he might make the best horse in the long run, if given more time.

We need a fairly good-sized pen and some cattle that aren't too rank. Follow one gentle cow around, and hold her in a corner. Then let the colt see what he has done. He's forced the cow into a corner, and he's holding her there. At this point the colt should be rewarded with a tidbit of some kind that he likes or, at least, with a friendly pat and a kind word. We must put across the point that we're pleased with him.

If all this goes well, perhaps we can give the colt a little more work. If the cow isn't too rank or fast, let her go down the fence a little, then get ahead of her and turn her back. At this point we're doing a little following, then actually blocking the cow when we pick her off the fence. This can give the colt a lasting impression of how to take the cow off the fence, and also teach him not to fear the fence while still working slowly with a gentle cow.

After a few passes the cow will generally stop. She isn't able to go anywhere, so she gives up. Let the colt stand facing the cow, reward him, and then slowly ride away or dismount to signify that the work is over. If we had continued to work this played-out cow, the colt would have been forced to go up very close to get any movement out of her. This could lead to a couple of bad results. The colt might get the idea that he should always work right on the cow, which could lead to charging, and the cow might gain the leverage to slip past the colt. Since a colt is easily discouraged, we don't want to lose cattle if we can avoid it.

A good place to teach a colt cow work is the round pen or bronc pen. One cow is in the pen. A round pen sixty-feet in diameter won't give the cow much room to run. She's as close to the fence as she can get. The colt can cut her off as a fighter might cut off his opponent in the ring. She has to do the traveling.

The rider can block the cow anytime he cares to by the angle he takes toward her. He can stop and roll the colt back over his hocks to turn the cow. This virtually eliminates all the useless running you'd have in a large arena or in the open.

The small pen gives the trainer a chance to work on a

Pal has gone around the calf, turned it back, and is jumping out to head it again.

colt's weakness. When I started Steel Helmet, he'd turn fine one way but would squat and then leap into the air the other way. We put one cow in the bronc pen and worked the horse slowly on his poor turn until he worked it as well as the other.

One thing many cutting-horse trainers neglect is to teach the colt just how to take a cow off the fence. If the colt runs to the fence to block, the cow can easily slip under his neck. If he learns to get around and face her on the fence, he'll make successful blocks. This can be practiced in the small pen, for neither cow nor horse has to do a lot of

133

running. Situations can be set up for practice. In the small pen the colt has a better chance of mastering a cow and less chance of learning about guarding the herd and charging a cow.

Some horses seem to walk through a herd naturally, as if easing through a mine field. Steel Helmet was tough about this because he'd been turned out with a couple of bulls and learned to chase them. When I tried checking pastures with him, he'd bounce up and down like a yo-yo, for he thought cattle were put on earth for him to chase.

There was no way I could get him simmered down in the pasture. It had to be done by practice, practice, practice in the pen with "doggy" cattle. I'd ride into the herd sitting alertly in the saddle. When I made my cut, I'd "sog" (sit way back, or sit heavily, in the saddle). He'd realize he was supposed to come out slowly.

But he had to be alert to the specific one I cut out, for I wanted him to stay with the particular one I first reined him at. Finally, I realized that I had to inspire him to work the way I wanted him to. When I rode in to cut, I mentally told myself that Steel would separate a cow quietly and alertly. When I could make myself *believe* that he would make a good cut, he did.

This is one reason the "pros" are hard to beat. They have confidence in themselves and their horses. The pro knows the horse will work a certain way and has no doubt about it. He wills the colt to enter the herd quietly, make an alert cut, drive the cow out the proper distance, and then set up to block.

The novice has no such ability to "psych" himself up. He sees some top cutters that he's about to butt heads with and tells himself that he doesn't have a chance. He's in a blue funk, nervous and upset. He relays this to his mount, and they have the disaster the fellow knew they'd have. The novice must learn mental preparation—a very tough lesson.

In a few instances I've had such a willing colt to work with that I've actually done a good job of cutting cattle in his first week of saddle training. In such cases that I was surprised and pleased with the colt's willingness and desire to please. Then I "just knew" he'd be in the right place at the right time, and he was.

With most colts, checking pastures is an excellent way to go. A rider will ride through a pasture, see some cattle and ride over to check them out for such things as pinkeye or hoofrot. He rides into the cattle and slowly moves one away from the others. She's OK. He stops, puts his hand on the colt's neck, and singles out another. This cow may want to be with her friends rather than move out, so the colt gets to make a couple of easy blocks.

The colt soon knows how to pussyfoot through cows in order not to get the whole bunch up and running. They may even find a sick cow that must be driven to a pen or roped and doctored in the pasture. I don't think it hurts a cutting horse's prospects one bit to have his rider rope heels off of him. All of this teaches him many things about a cow, makes him think. When he has it down pat, he can start his arena cutting.

Now, let's cut out a few cattle. We'll take the colt into the herd as easily as possible. We won't get technical or try anything tricky now; we'll pick out a cow who looks as if she will come out easily. After she's out, we'll let her go down the arena, and then reward the colt. We'll follow her out about forty feet. If she looks as if she might come back, we'll hold up the colt and block her, if possible.

Now, if this cow is rank, it's time to get off and fool around with the colt, letting the cow get back in the herd. There's no sense getting the colt beaten by the first cow he's cut out. But if you have taken out an easy cow, in all probability she will just amble across the pen and stand. If this is the case, we'll leave her alone and cut out a couple more. If the colt gets the idea of stopping and waiting for the cattle to come back, he has done very well. We'll plant the idea in his mind that after he takes the cow out a little way from the herd, he should stop and block the cow's return.

This now requires daily practice. The colt shouldn't be shown too many cattle at any one time—his interest may fade as he gets tired. How many weeks or months will this need to be practiced? It depends largely on how much interest and ability the colt shows. When the colt can cut out cattle without spooking the herd, when he can stop, wait, and block the cow's return, it is time to bring in help in the form of a "turnback" rider.

The turnback rider does not have to be a good cutting-horse man mounted on a good cutting horse, though it sure helps. Still, you can get along with a pretty sorry rider and horse as long as the rider has an idea of what you want and will follow your instructions.

When the cow is cut from the herd, she should be allowed to move out well into the arena before the turnback acts. He then tries (quietly) to put the cow back with the cows she just left. The rider on the colt can direct the turnback as to when to move in and when not to. An overzealous turnback man can foul you up with a green colt. As a general rule, the cutting horse should not move forward after he initially follows the cow out from the herd. He should just block, duck and dodge, and fall back to keep in working position.

It takes a little sense on the turnback's part to keep the cattle fresh and working as long as possible. He should fall back after bringing the cow to the cutting horse in order to give himself leverage and room to maneuver. If he is right

Ken Serco on Steel Helmet, blocking and falling back.

on top of the cow, the cutting horse will duck the cow past him; he'll lose the cow and have to go down the pen to get her and bring her back. This is a surefire way to sour cows and start them running. Running cows are sour cows, since they'll just run from one side of the pen to the other between the two horses, and nothing will be accomplished except sweating up the horses. Good help will keep cattle fresh and working much longer than will sorry help.

So, let's say we have a good turnback and our colt is coming along all right. Work might go something like this: The cow-cutter rides in back of the herd and around until he finds the animal he wants. The herd-holder holds the herd and/or rolls it by the cutter to help him make his

137

selection. The cow is cut out and eased from the herd. The cow trots out, and the cow-cutter follows her for about forty feet and stops to wait for the cow. The turnback brings back the cow, and she ducks and runs a few feet to get by the cutting horse that is right there, head to head. The cow sees she cannot get by, so she turns back down the pen. The turnback has fallen back maybe twenty feet, so he's in position to block the cow and return her to the cutting horse, and another head-to-head block is made.

When the cow gives up her attempt to regain the herd, the cutter dismounts or puts his hand on the horse's neck, backs up, and turns away, which allows the cow to re-enter the herd. This gives pretty fair play, and both cow and horse are getting good work. The cow finds that she can get back to the herd, and colt, by being stopped from working, has won the play.

Even if one cow is a good worker and helps the horse learn a lot, don't just work the same cow over and over. Cut out different cattle, work them right, and they'll work longer. Almost all cattle will finally sour for you, and there is little you can do to freshen them. A really doggy cow will just stand after she has been cut out, and this makes both the cutting and the turnback horses work too tight to the cow. This teaches the colt to work too close, and he will lose rank cattle. A running cow is sour; when a cow learns to run, the colt must also run to get with her. Then they all need to be reined. It does not take long for a good-feeling colt to decide that the working pen is a racetrack.

Once in a while we'll get a colt who really needs waking up. He'll lose cattle because he won't jump out and move, even though he is physically able and knows how to go about it. Since such a colt needs some persuasion, we'll use whip, spur, or both. Of course, you can't use a bat in a cutting

Ken and Steel working a good calf.

contest, but you should not train your horse at shows anyway; this is better done at home.

The colt will eventually become accustomed to spurs, so we'll use them sparingly, along with the bat. We want spurs to be a signal, not a punishment; too much spur will turn the colt into a tail-wringer or worse. A little touch with the spur coupled with a whack with the bat will teach him to jump out or go right in to pick a cow off the fence. Keep after him with the bat when you aren't at the shows, and he'll stay much more responsive to the spur.

139

The author on King of Clubs, trying to ride with the horse.

Don't continually peck at the colt with spur or bat, and leave him alone when he is doing all right. If we consistently reward him when he makes the right moves as well as punish him when he makes the wrong ones, it's easy to figure which he'll want to do. A reward can be a kind word or a friendly pat, even a piece of sugar. I have ridden colts that would become crestfallen at a harsh word. They would recognize a friendly word after completing a nice head-to-head block. We don't have to fall all over their necks to show our appreciation.

There is a close bond between a good cutting-horse man and his horse. If the rider just sits in the saddle and hangs on, he is doing nothing to help the colt. The rider should look at the chosen cow and lean his weight the way the colt should go, but he should ride straight up. The shifting of the weight is slight, not the overdone, sloppy job we often see. The colt is aided more by the *idea* of shifting weight than by two hundred pounds flopping all over his back.

If we ride in a lackadaisical manner, all slouched back, behind the horse every jump, and maintaining our seat by means of a death grip on the horn, the horse will do a sloppy job. If we aren't eager and helping, the horse won't be eager either. If we don't enjoy cutting cattle, we can't train cutting horses. We must know that the horse will work right, and then he will work right. The good cutting-horse man will make an average horse look good, while a sorry rider will make his horse lose cattle and do a poor job in general.

# 11. Understanding the Cutting Horse Rules

TRAINERS who have only a vague idea about how a cutting horse works should thoroughly acquaint themselves with the rules before attempting to train one. A copy of the rules can be obtained from the National Cutting Horse Association (NCHA). If you are serious about cutting horses, you should join the association.

Let's examine the rules and talk about them. These rules are the basis for judging all NCHA shows:

**Rule 1. A horse will be given credit for his ability to enter the herd of cattle and bring one out with very little disturbance to the herd or to the one brought out. If he (or the rider) creates unnecessary disturbance throughout his working period, he will be penalized.**

A horse must have training, sense, and a close mental sympathy with his rider to enter a herd quietly. The horse steps cautiously into the herd, pausing if the cattle start to mill around nervously. The rider picks the cow to be cut out and signals the horse. After being reined a time or two, the horse should know which cow his rider wants.

The rider needs much self-discipline for this. If he is the nervous type, he must put nerves aside and concentrate on the job at hand. If he is calm and cool and alert, chances are his horse will be too.

I talk to my horses a lot, and they know what "Whoa" and "Easy" mean. I can tell my horse, "Easy," and we will go into the herd. A little leg pressure and a touch of the rein indicate which cow I want. We ease the cow out and try to block easily and casually when the cow turns to re-enter the herd. The real play starts when the cow is out far enough for the turnback man to start working.

A contestant will judge his stock and try to select a cow that will offer good play for the horse. If he has to take the first one he comes to because his horse will not work the herd, he will always cut "traveling" cows that want to run instead of try to get back to the herd. These cows come out easily but show badly.

The way in which you cut out the selected animal is important. Cows should not be "chipped" from the herd. To chip one out, the rider would cut from the front, with his horse facing the back fence. He'd have to take, off the end, one that wanted to come out. In all probability, this cow would be a runner or a rank cow, one that would either run from fence to fence (showing no play to build points), or be so crazy that she'd lower her head and come through the horse to regain the herd.

Correct cutting procedure is carried out from the back of the herd. Whether you ride in from the corner or split the herd from the middle depends upon the number of cattle in the herd. When cutting from more than seven or eight cows, the herd should be split. It is always easier to cut from a small bunch than a large bunch, where the one you want tries to get lost in the crowd.

The speed of the horse in the herd must be correct for the kind of cattle you are working. This is another instance where close communion between horse and rider is necessary. Slow, herd-loving cattle call for a careful cut. Moving too slowly and cautiously can actually keep a cutter from making a cut, and he can be hung up in a tight herd for most of his working time.

The cutter should move to the back fence and, by reining a few times, signal to his horse which cow is desired. The horse should then see the cow and bring her out at the proper speed. The cow should be driven well out on the first cut to show that the horse can drive cattle. The next cut need not be driven so deeply. If any chipping of cattle is done, it should be the last cow, to ensure that you are working stock when time is called. Being caught in the herd when time is called is not a disaster, but most cutters feel that it is better to be out and working.

The herd holders will hold up the herd or move traveling cows past the cutter to allow him to pick out the cow of his choice. Usually the cattle will mill around when the cutter is in the herd. It is up to the herd-holders to contain the cattle. A horse moving too fast, however, will spook cattle and make the herd holders' task almost impossible.

At home, with only one rider to hold herd and turnback, he will hold herd, move the herd past the cutter for the cut, and then fall back to act as turnback when a cow has been cut out.

**Rule 2. When an animal is cut from the herd, it must be taken toward the center of the arena. If it goes down the arena fence, that is all right, but the horse should never get ahead of the animal and duck it back toward the herd to get more play, but should let the turnback man turn it back to him.**

When we first start our colt working cattle, we'll follow a cow, hold her in a corner and duck her back, because we are trying to get the colt to look at a cow. The colt, when learning to look at a cow, will push a doggy one with his nose, nip at her, and do other things we have no use for in a contest. His life work will be cow work, and he must learn all about the animal. Going past a cow and ducking her back off the fence teaches the colt to go in by the fence and pick off the cow. He needs plenty of this so that later in his career he will not be afraid to get right in when a cow is on the fence. Picking a cow off the fence is done all the time when working cattle on the range.

But once we start using a turnback, we'll discontinue this practice. From this point on, we follow contest rules. We bring the cow out, stop, and wait for the turnback to bring the cow back to us; we seldom deviate from this. Cow-cutting is, in part, watchful waiting on the part of both horse and rider.

Rule 3. A horse will be penalized 2 points each time the back fence is used for turn-back purposes, etc. If the cow gets far enough and deep enough to reach the back fence, the horse has missed a block or two and has almost lost the cow into the herd. Of course, a rider training a colt at home often uses the back fence with no special thought about its being either a good or bad practice. But as the colt progresses into a finished cow horse, he should gradually make better and quicker moves, and the back fence should be used less and less.

Back-fence stops are sometimes caused by overzealous turn-back men who keep pushing a rank cow back to the cutter.

Rule 4. If a horse runs into, scatters the herd, lanes or circles the herd against the arena fence, while trying to herd an animal, he will be penalized heavily.

This rule is often broken, especially by young, inexperienced horses. The situation is generally something like this:

The cow comes back to the herd fast and shoots by, or through, the cutting horse. He makes an attempt to head her, and, in his wild try to get where he is supposed to be, runs right into the herd and scatters the cows.

Or the cow outducks the cutting horse and gets by him. He overworks in an effort to head and loses the cow into the herd. It is only natural for him to want to get to his cow, even if the others happen to be in the way.

A colt that is a little slow with his stops and turns will generally lose the broken-field-runner kind of cow. He heads her, and she ducks by before he can set himself, jump, and start to head her again.

We cut a cow from the herd, and she leaves like an express train. The cow bounces off the turnback man and comes back like a rocket. The horse is between her and the herd. If he blocks her, she will hit him and go on through. This cow makes a bad show, because very few horses have the ability to stop her. A really brilliant horse might block, jump, and fly backward to block again, but most novice horses just aren't up to this kind of maneuver.

Such cattle at home will sour the colt and make him lose interest. He must win most of the time to keep up his interest, so we must choose cattle more suited to his style at first. Then he'll be ready for a really rank cow.

**Rule 5. If a horse turns the wrong way with tail toward animal, he will be disqualified for that go-round with no score.**

I once read an article in a horse magazine in which the author stated that if you wanted to make a cutting horse, you would never let him turn his tail toward a cow, while you would turn tail to the cow to make a reining horse. He said that it had taken him many years to learn this and that there were many good cowboys reared in the hills who had not learned this yet.

Hogwash! The only time you turn your tail to a cow is

when you are tangled in your rope and stuck fast in a barbed-wire fence.

Turning around on a cow causes you to lose her almost automatically and teaches the horse to work on the wrong end. The horse should plant his rear end and duck and dodge with the front end in motion. There is no question about this whatsoever.

## Rule 6. Reining and cueing penalties.

While training a cutting horse, we will rein him as little as possible, since we are trying to make him a self-worker. If we have to rein him very much at a show, we will be penalized right out of the money.

When at home, if you must rein or even pull the colt to get him into the correct head-to-head position, do it. At home it doesn't cost a cent. The horse must learn to be there, and you can't teach him that by letting him ramble at will anywhere he wants to go.

Since this rule deals with cues, let me mention a couple of cues I used to teach a horse to fall back when falling back is necessary to maintain working position. Many horses must be taught to back up to keep the working advantage; otherwise they will just let a cow work up on them farther and farther until she is so close they have lost the distance advantage, and then they lose the cow. When the colt learns to back up by himself, he will keep his leverage.

First, you obviously should have a good back-up on your colt. He must back up before he works cattle, but, even so, when we back him up to maintain leverage, his head will go up too high; he'll pay so much attention to our backing him that he will forget about the cow—and she will make it back to the herd.

We solve this by teaching our colt to back to a voice cue. To start with, we lean forward and tap him on the chest with a bat while saying, "Back," and backing him with the reins. Soon we will be able to back him with light taps and the vocal command without using the reins. We'll work on this until we will back by voice alone. Then we employ this in connection with cow work, and presto! our colt is backing to keep his working position with his head low and his eye on the cow. We use the vocal command for a while, but gradually the colt will learn what he's doing and will truly back up himself.

Some horses might get to falling off to the side (turning away from the bat). A backing collar might be the answer here. I take a piece of rope, tie a couple of knots in it, and loop it around the colt's neck. I fasten one end to the cinch by means of a strap and a snap so that the pull will be well down on his chest and not up on his neck. A well-reined horse will handle with this rig. Since the pull is down on his chest, he has little reason to raise his head.

Two training whips will really sharpen the back-up. A touch of the whip on the colt's shoulder will speed his back-up. A rider using two whips, one in each hand, can keep him constantly backing straight and fast.

**Rule 7. Riding with a tight rein through a performance will earn a penalty, the number of points lost to be determined by how often the offense was committed.**

Here is a quote from "General Information Regarding Cutting Horses" in the NCHA booklet: "One of the main essentials of a good cutting horse is that he works stock on a loose rein, the reins being used only when pulled up or stopped. Perfect cooperation and coordination between horse and rider is necessary."

The cutting horse must work on a very loose rein. His head must be down and free enough that he can block calves, goats, and low-headed cows. When a cow sees that head with the flattened ears and scary look, she is frightened into turning. A cutting horse can look mighty mean, but a tight rein can pull that look right off his face. If a horse doesn't have freedom of action, he can't work his best.

If we ride with a tight rein, the horse will be depending on us for his signals. When we add our own reaction time to that of the horse, we'll be too slow to rein at the right place and the right time when the chips are down.

I would like to offer a word of advice to loose-rein riders. Let's say I am working a horse and keeping the reins very loose. When I have to pull him up, I have to pull with my hand up high. This pulls the horse's head up, and he loses sight of everything but the moon, stars, and high-flying birds. The cow is gone. I am disgusted with the horse for losing the cow, but the fault is all mine. Here is a solution that will at least help when working at home:

Remember that low hands make a low head. I can check the colt with the hand low if I use both hands. Let's say I am holding the loose reins in my left hand, and I want to stop the horse. I can grab both reins in front of the saddle with my right hand and keep it down on the withers, letting the reins slip through it as I pull. This makes my right hand a sort of running martingale. The horse will flex his neck and bring in his nose, thereby being checked with no stargazing. He can still see cows and get working again in a much better fashion. By practicing this way at home, the horse won't be so likely to throw his head up when checked with one hand at a show.

The rider must use extreme care in handling his cutting horse. This loose-rein stuff is not much good when dry-working a horse. A slight contact with the mouth is best, but this means *feather* light. The horse can then get set to maneuver, which is not the case if the reins have a foot of slack one minute and are jerked up and back the next. The abrupt yank on the reins is always a surprise, and any horse will throw his head up in reaction to it.

**Rule 8. If a horse lets an animal get back in the herd he will be penalized 5 points.**

Sometimes it is virtually impossible to stop a crazy kind of cow from getting back into the herd, but there are three principal reasons why a green or average horse will lose a cow:

1. Not falling back or working too close. A horse must gauge cattle and be ready to fall back or jump back to maintain leverage. Here is the place to use the back-up command, given without reins.

Let's say we have picked a cow that comes at us and wants to charge through rather than turn back. She will come either fast or cautiously, and when the horse ducks one way to head her, she'll lunge forward and try to make it back to the herd before the horse can dodge back and get in position. The horse must then make up lost ground and get head-to-head. It was a mistake to cut out this cow in the first place, and the only wise thing to do is to get rid of her as soon as possible, without having a "hot" quit, which is always penalized heavily. If the cutter can make a successful block and turn her down the arena, that is the time to quit (often a wise turnback will allow this cow to slip through him instead of turning her back).

2. Working too close to the herd. When we cut a cow, we should follow her well into the arena before stopping to wait for the turnback. If the horse has his tail in the

Ken and Steel Helmet are almost cut down by a running calf trying to beat them to the herd.

herd, there's no place left to fall back to, and the horse will be working his cut from the middle of the scattered herd. This is heavily penalized.

Chances are that after a rank cow has been headed a few times, she will give up and turn toward the turnback man. We can then quit her and try a cow that shows better. But should she not quit, the horse will really have to buckle down and work to keep head-to-head with the cow and stay out of the herd. When there's no place to fall back to, the horse must make up for it with very fast work and correct anticipation of the cow's next moves. He needs some luck, too.

3. **Green horse.** If we have a good young horse started, he may make all the right moves but still not be fast and catty enough. He hasn't learned that he can speed up. He'll work right, but his turns and jump-outs will be too slow.

It takes time to make a cutting horse, and this colt should have a chance to work at home until he's speeded up. He should work cattle that he can master, and work only when he is fresh. If we ride five miles before working cattle, the colt will not be tired, but the fine edge will be gone. After his speed and handiness come to him, he might need a little preliminary work to make him steadier and more reliable, though this depends on the individual horse.

When we go into the herd with a horse that is a little fresh, he may make some mistakes, but he'll want to work because he wants the exercise. He can learn a lot about speeding up his turns in the few minutes he is still snorty.

If we give the colt plenty of time and patience and he still won't speed up, we'll have to resort to whip and spur. The colt should be familiar with spurs before working cattle. Otherwise we may use the spur to head a cow and succeed only in getting bucked down. I say this from sad experience.

**Rule 9. When a horse heads an animal and goes past it to the degree he loses his working advantage, he will be penalized each time he does so. If a horse goes by as much as his length, he will be assessed a heavier penalty. Unnecessary roughness, such as a horse losing his working advantage to paw or bite cattle, will be penalized.**

If we work the colt too fast, we may get him overworking. When he goes by a cow, she has the advantage of both speed and distance. I have ridden horses that went past a cow and had to turn and jump out very violently to get the cow

The author on King of Clubs, jumping hard to get back in position.

headed; then they'd pass the cow the other way and have to repeat the whole thing. They might not lose the cow, but they give the rider an exceedingly rough ride, and any judge will really tear apart such a performance.

Arena conditions may mislead a horse and make him miss his head-to-head position. A horse used to working cattle out in the hills will be fouled up when working in a disked-up arena or on sand.

The colt that goes by a little and has to jump back violently to head must be slowed down and taught to think. We can help him at home if he is light in the bridle and responds well to body aids. This gives the rider a lot to do—rein, cue, and shift body weight—but such things separate the trainers from the passengers.

At home when the colt has done a good job, get off him and fool around with him before he fidgets and tries to go to work on his cow. Let him know that he does not have to work all the time he is in the arena. When we relax in the saddle and show a lack of interest in working a cow, the horse should stand quietly. This might take a lot of mounting and dismounting, but the horse will get the idea. General cow work will also help, and tying up the horse (when all in a day's work) is beneficial. If the colt learns to work for all he is worth when he should work, and rest as well as he can when he is not working, we are doing a good job of making a real "using" horse.

If we buy a horse that overworks and has always done so, we have a tough proposition. The best thing to do is restart him on cattle, beginning with doggy ones. This will slow him down and teach him to really look at a cow and gauge her. Give him all-around cow work, cattle-driving, rope work, and plenty of riding. Reteaching a horse basic principles takes a lot of time and wet saddle blankets, but it's about the only way to get the horse to understand a cow.

There's a difference between overworking and setting up cattle. A horse should learn to set up his own cow, since the turnback rider won't do this for him at a show (if the turnback does set up all the cattle for the cutter, his horse is showing so much that the turnback gets looked at more than the cutting horse).

The cutting horse might run along with the cow a little, but he soon gets in front and turns her back. He does this every time she turns. If she's setting up well, she's ducking

The author on Wilda Boy, ducking and dodging.

and dodging while the rider is scoring points. If the horse just lopes along with the cow, waiting for her to turn, he's doing nothing and is scoring no points. If the turnback sets up the cow, he's "boxing her in" for the cutter.

The important reason for setting up the cow instead of relying on the turnback to box for you is that there's no turnback when you're actually cutting in a pasture or on the range. You'd run that ol' cow for miles if your horse wouldn't set her up and drive her out. The true cutting horse should be able to work as well in the pasture as in the cutting arena.

Sometimes when a colt is too slow or doesn't work in close enough to the fence, we'll lose the old temper and work him over too much. He'll become afraid of us and *really* overwork, or try to run off. It is then the same old story. Lay off the colt for a few days and show him much kindness. Take off your spurs and work him on slow cattle for a while. If he makes some right moves, show him kindness and reward him. If he's afraid, he'll watch his rider and not the cow.

When a colt or horse is too rough on cattle, I believe that it is often because he connects working a cow with getting spurred. Let's say that the horse comes in slow to pick a cow off the fence. We spur hard to get there in time. If we spurred this hard when the colt wasn't looking at a cow, he would run, jump, buck, or kick at the spur. Since he has the cow in front of him, he associates the spur with the cow and leaps in to strike or bite at the cow. After very much of this, the horse may become a regular "cow-eater."

Another example: We are riding drag behind a bunch of slow cattle. When we are right behind a cow, we hit the horse with a whip; he runs into or goes around the cow. If we hit him with spurs instead of a whip, he lays his ears back and bites the cow. Whenever possible we should

The author on King of Clubs. King of Clubs is eating the calf. He didn't do much of this. If he had, a snug bosal would have been used so that he couldn't open his mouth to bite.

lay off the spurs; the colt will then probably be a little less ready with his teeth.

CUTTING CUTTING COSTS

Friends, cutting cattle is fun. Training cutting horses is fun. Folks are missing fun that they could be enjoying because of what they have heard about the expense of maintaining a cow horse and cattle.

157

What makes it expensive? First, the cattle and the replacement cattle. Some people sour cattle in a couple of weeks. They they have to replace them. This means that they must buy and sell twenty to thirty cows twice a month. This gets to be mighty expensive.

Why do cattle sour so quickly? Overwork! If you're going to let everyone in the county work your cattle, they'll sour fast. If you enjoy having a lot of people around to work your cattle, you'll have to pay for it. Many enjoy this and can afford it. They buy fat two-year-olds, sour and take weight off them, and replace them at a loss.

Let's see how the poor boy can do it. First, buy young cattle, preferably poor ones. They'll grow while you're using them, even though they won't fatten up much. Give them good care (you might even make money on them). Worm them! No use feeding worms. Keep the flies off them. Put them in a horse stall and spray them fairly often.

If you have little pasture and have to feed, use economical local feed. Feed what is available. Check with some smart local cowman.

To keep these cattle working, work by yourself. There is always a joker in the deck, and a joker who runs cattle and plays "cowboy" will make cattle impossible to work, or sour. You and a herd-holder who can double for a turnback man are enough.

So, if your cattle feel good and you don't sour them with overwork, they should last quite some time, especially if you have but one cutting horse.

If your only horse is your cutting horse, you can get turnback help from someone on foot. A man who just stands down the arena and waves an arm once in a while can be a big help when your cows get too gentle to furnish much play.

The size of the arena is important. The larger the pen,

the fresher the cows will stay. Nothing sours cattle like working in a small, inside arena. You can gentle cattle inside in one session.

A big pen and/or pasture cutting will teach a colt to set up his own cattle. This is vital. A small pen will teach a colt to work off his hocks. The cow can't run as much in the small pen, so she will be more apt to duck and dodge. Since a horse really needs both kinds of work, it's not a bad idea to build two pens. The small pen should be forty to fifty feet wide and a hundred feet long. The larger pen should be about sixty-five feet wide and two hundred feet long.

This doesn't sound very wide, but when your colt must run back and forth to head running cattle, it'll seem much wider. I don't see much reason for a pen to be wider than sixty-five feet. I'd rather cut in a pasture than a really wide pen.

Pens to work in, though an initial expense, will last for a long time; so build good high ones. Often, cattle will be a little panicky when worked for the first time, and they are less apt to come out of a six-foot fence than a five-foot fence. After being worked a couple of times, practically all cattle will lose their initial fear.

So the pens are built and the cattle purchased. If you buy the cattle right, chances are they won't cost you much.

Now for the horse. I hope you buy a good gelding. A gelding, not having sex to worry about, makes a good, reliable, ever-ready cow horse. Buying a colt with "cow in his pedigree" will help. Of course, training your own horse will help financially. If you need to take the colt to a trainer for a few months, perhaps you could have him going well enough for the trainer to go right on with him.

Just a word about cutting clubs. There are people who buy cattle together and have regular cutting sessions. This is a "share-the-expense" deal that works very well under certain circumstances. The main thing is that you shouldn't join such a group and expect to train your cutting horse at the sessions. You should train him at home and take him to such a cutting to cut under actual contest conditions. If everyone who joins such a group goes there to train his horse, bedlam will result. Cattle will be immediately soured, horses will be spoiled, and ill feeling will be the end result.

For instance, one rider will want to the right thing. He'll go into the herd, cut a few cattle, use no more than regular contest time, and ride out satisfied. Another will go in, chase cattle for fifteen minutes, and ruin things for everyone else. Make sure before joining such a group that you are not joining up with a bunch of "heel flies."

Abide by definite rules. Run a get-together like a regular cutting. It needn't be judged, but limit the time in the herd to two and a half minutes. The "wild ones" won't like this, and they'll stop coming. The people who appreciate a nice session will come regularly. These clubs should just simulate a regular contest and no more. If run right, these get-togethers are a fine thing, and I wish every town had such a place available.

Owning a pleasure cutting horse is a hobby. All hobbies cost a little money. By keeping costs down, cutting will cost no more in the long run than golf or photography.

# 12. Accident Prevention

ONE of the things you learn when you raise horses is that some of them are suicide prone. When I managed Meridian Meadows, we had many Pasos die over the years. This was a modern, well-maintained operation. Perhaps listing some of the things we found to be horse killers might help others.

A major horse killer is colic. The horse's digestive system is sensitive. If he gets indigestion—gas, a gut ache—he's apt to roll. When the intestines are distended with gas, they may not roll with the horse, and we have a "twisted gut," a torsion. Though expert veterinary surgery has saved some such horses, most die or have to be "put down" to relieve them of their intense pain.

All feed must be carefully observed. Hay should "go through the sweat" before being fed to horses. If it's baled when the moisture content is too high, it may mold. *Before* mold shows as mold, however, it's extremely toxic. If a horse eats hay that is prone to mold, he may exhibit symptoms of colic but is being robbed of oxygen in his blood. He may actually suffocate. So it's best to wait a couple of weeks before feeding new hay. Then, if it's moldy, you can spot and smell the mold and, of course, discard it.

Sweet feed has a tendency to heat up and mold in hot, humid weather. Inspect it carefully before feeding it. Oats and bran are better hot-weather foods than sweet feed.

Worms, especially strongyles (bloodworms), are a major factor in deadly colic cases. Too often we simply worm the horse a couple of times a year and think we're safe. The manure of the horse should be checked quite often for worm infestation. I've written several articles about "do it yourself" checking, which isn't as good as having a veterinarian do it but a damn sight better than not checking it at all. Fecal checks tell us when horses need worming, and they'll save the lives of most of the horses that otherwise would die of colic (my opinion).

I don't believe as much in worms becoming immune to various wormers as I do in the failure of these wormers to kill worms "hibernating" in the intervascular system (again my opinion). You can worm to kill available worms, worm two weeks later to kill the new hatch, and consider your horses worm-free. In a month or so, however, new worms will slip out of "hibernation" in the arteries and blood vessels, and your horse is wormy again. Periodic fecal checks tell you the up-to-date worm situation.

Foundering ruins rather than kills. Study a veterinarian textbook for the complete scoop. Overeating—getting into the feed shed—and drinking a lot of water when hot are the main roads to founder. Horses *can* founder on grass or special plantings, such as millet.

Your veterinarian should be consulted about necessary shots. These are usually given in spring, and they protect the horse against sleeping sickness and tetanus. Other shots, such as those for flu, rhino, lepto, and so on, are given when needed. In mosquito-fly country, unprotected horses should be treated with repellant. We live in such an area, and the horses on my place live in screened-in stalls.

## HOW HORSES ARE INJURED AND KILLED

Pastures mean fences. I've seen many horses killed and crippled from pasture fences. One morning back in 1958 I checked pastures on the outfit I was riding for and found a two-year-old gelding lying on the ground surrounded by a sea of blood. His whole front quarter was almost sawed off. He'd been pastured directly across a fence from horses in another pasture. Field fence with a strand of barbed wire on top was the killer. He'd reared up, gotten a leg over the fence, and charged back and forth between fence posts. Blood and hair on the wire told the story. The barbs acted like a meat saw.

Could we have prevented this deadly accident? Yep, an electrified wire, sticking out a foot or so from the fence, would have made him leery of the fence. Of course, horses have been killed from an improperly constructed electric fence. When the instructions say to use a six-foot bronze rod for a ground, *use it.*

Whole herds of horses have been killed when a horse standing against a fence was hit by lightning. The lightning runs down the whole fence line, killing all horses up against it. A few iron posts would help to ground the lightning, a few horses might be killed, but most of the herd would be saved.

During a terrible storm at Meridian Meadows, four mares and three colts took shelter in the small shed. The other colt was close by. Lightning hit the shed, and all were killed. Moral? Install lightning rods! All the buildings on my place have professionally installed lightning rods. It cost me more than a thousand bucks, but it was money well spent, for we have thunderstorms here that are hard to believe.

I use a cheap field fence here. If a horse sticks a foot in it and jumps backwards, the stays break and the horse is loose. When a fence is wrecked in a few places, we cut the bad stuff out and replace it. I have a strand of smooth wire on top. The horses are kept in stalls rather than pastures and are grassed about an hour each day. We're here watching them when they're turned out. Get the idea?

Are board or pipe fences safe? Heck, no! I've seen horses and colts get stuck under them. They sometimes fight and die if no one's around to help them. Hurricane fence is about the safest fence you can use. It's heavy-duty stuff with woven wire running back and forth at very close intervals. You see such stuff around prisons and movie stars' outfits. Such a fence, say eight feet high, would be fairly safe, though I'm sure some horses would eventually find some way to kill themselves on it.

I've seen gates kill horses. The horses caught their necks between gate and post, then sat back and hanged themselves. I once measured a gap where a colt had hanged himself and found the opening to be less than two inches wide.

Marquesa de Medellin, a fine Paso mare, wanted to rub off some winter hair and picked a forked tree to rub on. She caught her head, plunged back, and hanged herself. The boss had a crew go over his seventeen hundred acres and cut the forks out of all the trees in the horse pastures. This made the horses think of other ways.

Dama got into deep mud in a pond, struggled, and died of a heart attack.

Those who fail to remove halters before turning their horses out are asking for it. It's a major method for killing horses. A mare rubs on a post, catches the halter, rears back, slips, and hangs herself on the post. Farnam markets a halter that comes apart at such times. Better yet, don't turn horses out with halters on them.

We get a lot of questions about how to catch horses in a pasture, especially when they have no halters on. I think that a guy who can afford a horse can doggone sure afford to build a small trap for catching horses. Build it around the feed trough, water tank, etc. Use such treats as grain for a reward when the horses do allow themselves to be caught. They'll be easier to catch next time.

Horses have explosive tempers and get "tiddled" off at each other. A horse can be run into and through a fence. When you do use a small trap, be right there to straighten out problems, and be very careful when you go into the trap to catch a certain horse. You can get kicked yourself. I feel safe when I have a lariat with me, for horses respect it.

When building a trap, make sure you don't fence in a narrow space where horses can get trapped and savaged by other horses. Give them room to escape. When you build a small trap, make two gates, and be sure both are open when you don't want to trap a horse. A horse trap is deadly *if one gate is shut.* Paint a sign and fasten it somewhere on the trap. It should say, "Keep Both Gates Open."

The best trap is a bronc pen about forty feet square. Drive horses into it, and you have them. Of course, some are hard to catch in such a big pen unless you can rope. If you *can* rope a horse in a pen, you seldom have to.

When folks buy automatic waterers, they can be buying horse killers. An animal can fall into a pasture tank, making the water so foul horses won't drink it. If you don't check your water tanks daily, your horses could be dying of thirst.

Stall waterers are just as bad. A horse can drop his manure in his waterer. He won't drink and can go very thirsty, so dry in fact that he'll founder when he has a chance to drink his fill of fresh water. The results can be founder, colic, or death.

The automatic waterer can malfunction. A clogged part means no water for the horse. Check daily.

The very first day I worked for Charley Araujo, I noticed a couple of fillies with very bad dysentery. The watery fecus was shooting out ten feet. I immediately checked their water and found that a salt block had fallen into the tank. I removed the block, drained and cleaned the tank, and refilled it. Then I made sure the fillies didn't drink too much fresh water all at once. They were all right the next day. Charley's neighbor had been caring for the horses while Charley was away, and he hadn't checked carefully enough.

We feed hay a half hour before we feed grain. This gets the digestive juices flowing and prepares the horse's system for the more potent grain. This takes time, but it's time well spent.

Our major grain is oats, and some bran is always added. We find that horses used to sweet feed will eat our ration if we add a little sweet stuff to the cooler oats and bran. I buy one thousand pounds of crimped oats, three hundred pounds of sweet feed, and one hundred pounds of bran for my feed order. We try to use this up so it'll all finish at the same time. Rather than mixing in huge quantities, we mix what we need each day to ensure that the bran and sweet feed are evened out with the oats.

Most common wood barns like mine have nails working loose, sticking out, and so on. Boards with nails in them and old pieces of farm machinery continually work up out of the arenas. A person must train himself to observe and correct such conditions.

If a nail starts working loose in a board, most folks just pound it back in (me too). But it'll just start working out again. The nail should be removed and hammered in at a different place. If you cut the points (or blunt the points) of these nails, they won't split wood. If the wood isn't split, the nails won't work out as easily.

ACCIDENTS WHILE HANDLING HORSES.

We hear about and see more serious accidents that are associated with tying up horses than any other aspect of horse handling. Why? Because no horse, no matter how well-trained, is immune from flying back on a tie rope and breaking either halter, lead, post, rail, or his own neck. When an animal resorts to flight as a natural instinct, and when that animal has great size, weight and strength, pulling back to escape is as natural as eating, drinking, and breathing. If a person says his horse hasn't pulled back and broken something, I answer that he hasn't *yet.*

It's easy to tie up and hold a colt or yearling. When a strong, twelve-hundred-pound horse tries to break loose, something's got to give. To hold such a horse, special equipment is needed.

I'll bet I've read a dozen magazine articles in a year about how various trainers teach horses to stand tied. The usual formula is, "strong halter, strong rope, and strong post or tree." The trainer will spook the horse to make him lunge back. When he can't break loose, he finds himself trained and never gives any more trouble. Not so. If something scares the horse in the future, he'll fly back no matter how well-trained he is.

We read so much opposing advice on this subject that I'm sure it's almost impossible for the novice to know what to do. You must decide for yourself whose advice you care to follow. If I had to agree with another writer-trainer about tying up horses, I'd pick Ed Connell's advice as being most nearly in agreement with *what I've found to be the best way.* Ed says never tie a horse with an unbreakable halter; it's better to have a loose horse in the barn than a dead horse in the barn.

A halter fits back of a horse's ears. The horse is very delicate where his head connects to his neck. If the pull is at that point, the horse can break or dislocate his neck.

If the pull is six or more inches back on his neck from his ears, there is far less chance of injury. Ed Connell broke colts to stand by using a strong rope to tie a gunny sack around the neck and then running the rope *through* the halter.

I agree and disagree with this. The idea is fine, but I've never had much luck rigging the gunny sack. My knots (clove hitches) have pulled off, or something else has gone wrong. A strong, soft foot rope (used for scotch hobbling) is my pick. I use a marine bowline knot around the horse's neck and run the rope through the halter.

Rope can be tied around the horse's cinch area, run between the front legs, and drawn up through the halter. Old-timers really liked this one, but I've yet to see it correct a halter-puller. It always makes a horse too sore to ride.

When I tie the rope around the horse's neck, I often hook him to an inner tube attached to my snubbing post. No horse can combat the effect of rubber that will stretch but continue to pull back. The stretch softens the pull when he does set back, and there's less chance of injury.

But the tied-up horse should *never* be left alone. He can fight, fall, and *hang himself.* The trainer *must* be right there and should *always* carry a sharp knife. You can't get any knot untied with the weight of the horse on the rope. Don't even try! Cut the rope pronto!

Is there any safe way to tie a horse? Nope. Probably one of the safest ways is to use the ol' stake-out rope. The long, soft, thick rope is tied around the neck (bowline knot), run through the halter, and fastened to a weight, such as a log or a big tractor tire. The horse can pull such a weight a little ways but not far. The danger? The weight can catch on something and be immovable. An open pasture is the thing. Of course, the horse can catch a foot through the halter and wreck himself, so even such a tie-out halter shouldn't be the unbreakable kind. The horse can be trained to be staked out by tying a rope to a strap around a front ankle. The end is usually tied as high as one can reach, to a small tree that has some give to it. Don't just go out and try this, however. The horse has to be trained to it, and hobble training is very good as a start.

Personally, I don't tie up horses unless the owner specifically asks for such training. If I *have* to tie one up, I use the snubbing post and inner tube. I usually use hobbles and a sideline for restraint.

Folks who interrupt their horses' feeding schedules can cause havoc by making their horses barn sour or pasture sour. It's a real problem. People have limited times to ride and the horses must put up with it.

I used to hate this. While working for wealthy folk, I'd have to work horses for them during their predinner cocktail break. They didn't give a damn if it was feeding time or not.

A horse has one big thrill in life, and that's eating. If a person enjoys drinks and a great meal, the horse enjoys his grain ten times more. The human may eat late and not be bothered by it, for he's made arrangements to eat later and knows that he won't go hungry. The horse has no such information and gets very upset when he's *singled out* to be worked while the other horses eat. This makes the horse so nervous and upset that he's very prone to colic when he does get his food.

We should think how being very nervous and upset affects us. A man who's in danger of losing his job, who is worried about the job loss, selling the house, moving to another location, or just being unemployed, will probably get severe indigestion if he tries to eat. In fact, such a situation can bring on a heart attack.

If the rider has a big fight with a horse before feeding time, the horse may colic. Some years ago, one of my apprentices had a fight with a colt about four in the afternoon. He yelled, slapped, and spurred the colt. Sure enough, the colt colicked and we had a night of it getting him straightened out.

The horse shouldn't be worked prior to or right after feeding. Given a choice, I'd work the horse after feeding.

# 13. Handling Stallions

THE day was a hot one. I'd fed and cared for thirty horses I was working with and had to take care of the old stallion. His stall was a mess. He was dirty and needed attention pronto.

Eagle View Chief, an old Saddlebred stallion, was somewhat rank to handle until ridden. I entered his stall, snapped a lead rope to his halter, and tied him to a ring in the wall. Before long I had the stall cleaned and bedded. Time to clean up the horse.

I curried and brushed Chief's offside and stepped under his neck to get around to the near side. He pounced on me like a lion and grabbed my left hip in his sharp old teeth.

The stud shook me as a cat would shake a mouse. Finally my hip and Levis tore loose, and I flew through the air across the twenty-foot stall, hitting way up near the haymow. It was a long fall down to the floor. I saw the horse lunge at me, coming with wide-open mouth between his forelegs, straight for my head. Thank God for the strong halter and lead, which jerked him up short of his goal.

Looking down at my hip, I almost got sick. What was left of it was jerking and quivering. A six-inch circle of flesh was missing. White bone and blood showed in the fleshless area. This was the first time a horse had ever tried to wipe me out, and Chief had done a good job of it. I still wear the scar.

When I moved to the high country of Colorado as the manager-trainer of a large horse ranch, I was told that two of their stallions were notorious man-haters. One horse would attack anyone who tried to whip him. A former employee was so told. He laughed at this information, took up a whip, and went after the horse. He had to be pulled out of the stall and packed to the emergency ward. This horse was never any problem to me, since I don't whip horses.

The other horse tolerated certain people and, for no apparent reason, hated others. He'd seriously bitten the owner and the owner's son. He hated one ranch hand but liked the irrigator. I seemed to have the proper vibrations, for he never made any bad gestures toward me. I had it in my mind that the people he seemed to hate had done something to him before my time.

One evening some friends came to dinner. Before eating, I gave them a tour of the barn. A horse-loving lady went into the stallion's stall with me to get a better look at him. He leaped at her, mouth open and ears flat back. Without thinking much about it, I jumped in front of her. The horse slid to a stop with his head on my shoulder and glared at her. I advised her to back out of that stall *right now.* She'd never seen that horse before.

This proof made it plain to me that you don't have to do anything to a horse to earn his animosity. Perhaps someone with the same smell, vibrations, or aura had given him cause for hate.

There are no real rules for handling stallions. If a stud makes up his mind to get you, he will, *sometime.* He has twenty-four hours a day to brood about it, and the sparks of a small injustice can build to a roaring inferno of horsehide filled with fury. A person has little chance then.

A strong, mature stallion can hold his own against any animal on this continent. Man is puny compared to him. At first man's hobbles and other ropes confuse him, for he can't seem to fight back, but he'll figure out ways to get even when a person is off guard. Not all stallions have this "brio" to lay for a man. A horse handler needs to figure out what kind of a stallion he has. If you have a stallion who isn't tuned in on your wave length, better swap him for another while you still can.

The stallion handler should really like horses. He should never abuse a horse. If he does have to punish a stallion, he should do so without anger, for the horse understands mental attitude.

The novice horseman always looks for set formulas about training, breeding, stallion handling, and so on. The ol' pro knows, or should know, that each horse is an individual. There are many ways to take care of the same situation. I've worked north, south, east, and west. Horses are handled differently in all parts of the world, and there's much to be learned from each place.

But if we must look for a general formula on this one particular subject, we must say that stallions are prone to nip and bite. They're handier with the front hooves than the back ones. A stallion thinks fast. His mind is always in high gear. His patience is short.

A fine stallion is purchased. Since he's so valuable, the owner wants him to look nice and spends a lot of time brushing and rubbing him. This is all right for a little while, but the stud gets tired of standing for all this grooming and nips the owner. The owner whips the stallion, for he's heard you can't let a stud get away with anything. The horse starts packing a grudge.

I don't believe in doing all that grooming. I'll get a stallion cleaned up enough so that there's no dirt under the saddle. Then I'll work him. If the weather permits, I'll wash the horse after his ride and turn him into a sandy lot to roll. If I do have to groom him, I'll do it quickly.

The folks who pack a buggy whip and lay it on for the

slightest misbehavior have ruined a lot of stallions. Some hotshots handle their colts in such a fashion and sell them about the time the horse starts thinking revenge. When that horse sees a whip, he'll be ready to blow up all over his new owner.

So, how does one handle a stallion for grooming, saddling, washing the genitals, and so forth? The stallion is an awesome hunk of fighting machinery. I've seen a thousand-pound horse lift a twelve-hundred-pound mare so that all four of her hooves were off the ground. This horse became provoked because the mare kicked at him repeatedly. He grabbed her by the neck, reared up, and waltzed her around for at least a minute before I could rope and drag him away from her. A stallion in temper is a lot like the "Incredible Hulk."

Since a stallion bites, make a snug, wire noseband for him. Slip it on under or over the halter. It doesn't hurt him if he doesn't try to bite. This is much more sensible than the old "nail in a board, hold it so he can hit it if he bites" routine. Or the cigarette to burn his nose with.

With the wire noseband, he punishes *himself* each and every time he tries to bite. Before long he'll realize that such attempts hurt, and he'll stop trying. The trainer has no reason to lose his temper, so the horse isn't whipped or put "on the prod" by sensing the anger of the man.

So, we've taken care of the biting, but he can still strike, kick, and jump around. It's best to educate him to hobbles and sideline. With such restraints on him, about all he can do is to fall on a person.

Most of today's colts are easy to hobble, for they've had their hooves handled and trimmed since birth. The really rank colt, wild off the range, would be forefooted, but we're not concerned with that now. Sometimes a fairly rank one has to be blindfolded before the hobbles can be put on. If the horse is bad about kicking or striking, go with the blindfold.

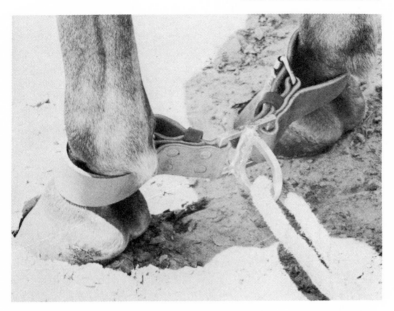

Hobbles and special D ring welded on.

A lot of trainers scotch-hobble (tie up a back foot). I use it once in a while, but a kicking horse will jerk his neck so much he'll fight all the more. The sideline, like the wire muzzle, doesn't bother the horse as long as he's behaving himself.

There are a lot of hobbles on the market, but I've had no luck with anything I could buy. I've designed my own rig that suits me. The hardware is made by a local welder. The hobble straps are made of nylon webbing. I burn holes in the nylon webbing for the buckle tongue and sew around them for reinforcement. I also use strong leather.

A lot of trainers use folded burlap sacks for front hobbles. These are fine if you're smart enough to keep them on a bronc. When I've tried to use them, the burlap has stretched,

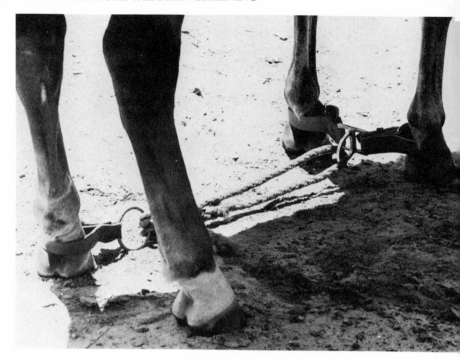

Hobbles and sideline.

allowing the bronc to pull free. I consider this a good way to get a foot in the face.

The hobbles on the market are too flimsy, too rough on the horse, or too hard to put on and take off. I trust what I make. When the bronc is trying to take your head off with his front hooves, you'd better be able to trust your gear (or know how much you *can* trust it).

I hobble the front legs and sideline one or both hind legs. When teaching the colt to be good about having his front legs handled, I secure one front leg to both back legs. He can't jump around or strike much. Then I handle the free leg. Taking time to handle hooves pays off in the long run.

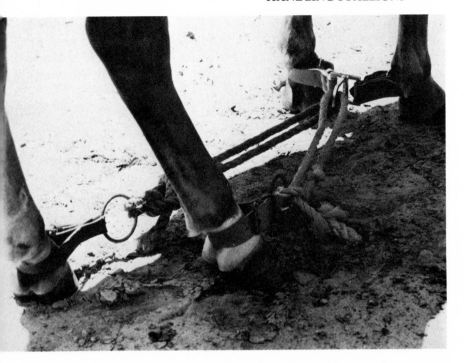

Hobbles and double sideline. When trimming hooves, you can release one leg at a time to work on it. This rig makes good breeding hobbles when the rope is fastened to one back-foot strap and run through the D ring back to the other back-foot strap.

If the horse really fights the hobbles, he may get a little sore on the outside of his pasterns. I hobble the pasterns, for there's less chance of tendon injury than there is in going around the cannon bones. If the horse learns his lessons and is a little sore next day, he can then be hobbled up on the cannons so that salve can be rubbed on his sore places.

A man once called to ask my advice about how he should

handle his stallion. The horse gave him plenty of trouble at breeding time. I told him to forget the whip and reward the horse for a good job. He asked how he should reward him. I suggested giving him something he enjoyed eating, such as carrots and apples.

The procedure would go like this: The mare would be teased, washed, have her tail wrapped, restrained, and the stallion would be brought up. The stallion should be "ready" (erect penis) before being brought up to the mare. Many handlers whip a horse to keep him back until he's ready. If he's whipped, he'll think about the whip rather than the mare, and he won't get ready.

I told the man just to hang on and circle the stallion until he was ready to breed. Then he should stop the horse, give him a reward as best he could, and immediately take him to the mare. Upon servicing the mare, he should be backed off, praised, and rewarded again.

The man wrote to me later. He said that he'd thought this was the craziest advice he'd ever heard, but, since he had asked for "expert" advice, he'd give it a try. My procedure worked perfectly for him, and the horse was breeding happily, promptly, correctly, and safely almost immediately.

When I first tried this method, I had to handle a very strong, young stallion who was "faster than a speeding bullet and able to leap tall buildings at a single bound." I was afraid I'd never be able to control that horse. I knew better than to whip at him.

Arthur Konyot used whips, but he rewarded horses for everything. I'd never used feed as a reward until I met Konyot. It dawned on me that I might be able to handle this torpedo of a stud if I used a reward. I had to think of something right away, for we had a bunch of mares to breed.

The colt teased a mare until she was ready. We prepared her for breeding, and a helper stood at her head. I slipped a California hackamore on the stud, tied up the reins, and gave him a tidbit. Then we went outside to the mare.

The young horse sensed what he should do and started getting prepared. When he was ready, I patted him and gave him a reward. I led him to the mare. He reared up, mounted, and serviced her promptly. When he finished, I backed him off, rewarded him, and put him up. From then on he was a calm breeder, very easy to handle.

We must have started twenty young stallions at breeding mares during my stint at Meridian Meadows. These young Pasos had no idea what they were supposed to do but, they went at it with reckless abandon. We used patient old mares who would put up with such foolishness.

A young stud might lunge and grab a mare around the neck with his front legs. I'd pull him down, jerk him around a little, wait until he was ready, and try to direct him to the right end. Before long those young stallions knew all about it, and they would be easy to handle.

I try to teach a stallion to watch out for himself. This takes knowledge of mares and stallions. I want a stallion to protect himself when turned out with a mare who might kick him, and the only way to do this is to actually turn him out with a kicky mare. The stallion should be knowledgeable about breeding before this is ever done. Some stallions rush a mare so blindly that this practice is impractical.

Why would anyone turn a stallion loose with a bunch of mares? Because some silent-heat or hard-to-breed mares can be "settled" only by catching them at the proper time with no humans present. The stallion knows when to breed such mares. I believe that running a stallion with mares is a good way to have a really high conception rate. At Meridian Meadows, the stallion Hilachas settled almost all the mares when he was used as the "clean-up" stallion.

It was our practice to hand-breed mares to various stallions during the spring of the year. Then we would wait a couple of months and turn Hilachas loose with the mare bunch. He would find and settle those tough mares that we'd had no real luck with. He never received so much as a scratch from being turned out with them.

Trying to fool Hilachas was about as chancy as trying to fool Mother Nature. When he came to us from Colombia, we rode him every day. But he was suffering shock from the airplane ride and from leaving his old environment. He was a breeding stallion, not a saddle horse, and he tried to tell us this by bucking harder each day. In a couple of weeks we were wondering if we'd be able to stay on him much longer.

One day I grew weary of his bucking. I threw him and tied him down. After this was over, I saddled, mounted, and took him out for a long ride. No more bucking.

But in a few days we had a mare to breed. I led Hilachas to the mare, who was all hunched up, waiting. Hilachas looked off into the distance, ignoring the ready mare.

About that time a lawyer friend dropped in to say hello. I asked him to lead Hilachas up to the mare. My helper and I both hid ourselves. When Hilachas could no longer see us, he serviced the mare.

For weeks we'd put mares in the run with Hilachas. He'd look for us and would never go to the mare until he was satisfied that we were nowhere around. Finally he decided that we had no more intentions of riding him, and he got over this quirk.

I could never lie to Hilachas and retain his trust. When we had a mare for him to breed, I'd go in the stall with a lariat and ask, *"Quire la yegua,* Hilachas?" (Do you want a mare, Hilachas?) I'd hold an open loop, and he'd stick his head into it. We'd go to the mare. He knew she'd be no bother, for I wouldn't lead him up to a rank one.

If we had a kicky mare for him, I'd lead him to the pen

where she was turned loose. Then the lariat would be slipped from his head. I'd say, "Peligroso, Hilachas" (Danger, Hilachas), and he'd circle her warily, waiting to see how she'd act. If he had to work on her to make her stand, he'd do so.

When we had no mares for him but wanted to turn him out for some grass, I'd approach the same way and ask him if he wanted grass. He'd willingly let me catch him. But if it was time for hoof trimming or shots, I'd go into the stall and say nothing. Hilachas would then tear around, trying to get away from me. I'd rope him, fight awhile, and do to him what had to be done.

We had one mare who was very peculiar. Though she'd appear ready to be bred and would conceive easily, she'd usually raise some kind of ruckus during the breeding. She'd fight restraints like a wildcat, so I decided to let Hilachas do it his way.

To be a little careful, I saddled a good rope horse, mounted, and waited in the seventy-foot-square pen while a helper brought Hilachas.

The stallion approached the mare warily, sniffed her, squealed, struck at some air, and sniffed again. The mare squatted and emptied out. She had the dazed, far-off look of a mare ready to be bred. All the signs told Hilachas that she was ready, so he mounted her.

Wham! She kicked him. I cocked my loop and rode in, but I couldn't find the horses in that huge cloud of dust. Something was going on, but I couldn't tell what it was. When the dust settled, Hilachas was dismounting. The mare had been bred, but she had three deep gashes on each side of her neck that ran halfway down her back. As I said, you didn't want to fool Hilachas.

When we deal with so much intelligence, we should recognize it and handle stallions accordingly. The whip doesn't make handling the horse one bit safer, and it can get you into big trouble. When the handler likes the stallion, respects his intelligence, and cooperates with the horse, he'll be far better off.

When I handle a stallion, I want room to maneuver. Using a short lead shank to take a horse to a mare doesn't let the handler get far enough away from the action. The stallion may strike, if only at the air. This is natural. It's his way of showing the mare how macho he is. Don't whip him for it.

The California hackamore and the twenty-two-foot mecate are ideal for this purpose. Enough wraps should be taken on the back of the hackamore to make a snug fit. The stallion can then nip the mare a little, but he can't really bite her.

The reins are tied up around the horse's neck. They don't have as much give to them as a fiador does. I have more confidence in them. If I used a fiador, I'd still tie the reins up. After the reins are adjusted on the noseband, there's about twelve to fourteen feet left for a lead.

If the horse really misbehaves, such as lunging at the mare before he's ready to breed, he can be ground-doubled and pulled away. He can be doubled back and forth until he stands. The long lead allows the handler to stay well back from those flashing front hooves.

All sorts of things happen when you handle a lot of stallions and mares. The most common thing to go wrong is to have the stallion get a front foot over the lead rope and get loose. For this reason I like a pen, such as a fifty-foot-square breaking pen, for breeding. I'll always have a lariat with a loop already built in it lying where it's handy to grab in a hurry. The ready lariat has saved the day for me many times.

I should say a few words about the mare to be bred. I don't care for breeding hobbles. The mare can still run and plunge in them. It makes her like a tank without a driver if she gets excited. I've seen pens quickly emptied of people when a mare broke away from the handlers while she was wearing breeding hobbles.

A twitch will restrain some mares, but you can't count on it. If the stud spooks her, she'll jump forward. The guy holding the twitch has to turn loose, and the mare is un-restrained.

Tying up a front foot (strapping it up) is a poor restraint. The mare tries to balance herself and usually goes down when the stallion mounts. It puts way too much strain on one foreleg. I've used this method and have released the foreleg when the stud mounts. That's the way it should be done, but, again, you then have no restraint on the mare during the breeding. They sometimes kick as stallions dismount.

Scotch-hobbling one hind foot of the mare is a pretty good practice. The foot is pulled forward, but the rope is long enough that the mare can still support her weight with it. She can't really kick with the free foot for the scotched hoof is too far forward for proper balance. The rope pulls on the neck, however, and can cause a good many mares to fight.

I like the hobble-and-sideline rig the best. There is no pull or stress on a mare so long as she stands. She can't rear or strike. Both back legs are sidelined, with the rope running through the D ring of the hobble hardware. She can still step around a little with her back legs and move to brace herself, but she can't kick.

The procedure goes like this: The mare comes in heat and is teased by a stallion. Ideally, most mares are bred about the fourth day of their period, if springtime is breeding time. The mare will accept teasing readily. She'll hump up and empty out. The urine will be more milky-looking than usual.

The mare is then restrained. Her genitals are washed with antiseptic soap and water. Her tail is wrapped with a clean bandage.

The stallion is brought to the vicinity of the mare. He's restrained, and his breeding apparatus is likewise washed with antiseptic soap (available from a veterinarian) and water. The hobbles are removed from the stallion. He's taken to the mare, and he services her. Afterwards the stallion should again be washed. Before breeding, all trace of soap must be rinsed away, for it will kill sperm.

The mare won't expel the semen if the service has been performed at the right time. A cool bath, however, will stop her from horsing and straining, so I think it's a good idea.

Though a mature stallion can service quite a few mares a day, the services should be limited to keep his sperm count up. Most mares that are "right" can be settled adequately by two services.

A lot of folks who read this will have no confidence in what I've said about handling stallions. They'll still act as though the stallions were lions in a ring and they were the lion tamers. Other people will have open minds and will accept this different way of handling stallions. It's for this latter group that this has been written.

# 14. Discipline Without Spoiling

THERE are reasons why humans spoil horses. Neither humans nor horses are all-wise. We are both good and bad. We are both intelligent and stupid. The most willing horse makes mistakes. The trainer who possesses great ability, experience, and knowledge also makes mistakes.

Humans and horses are very much alike. But maybe because of the position and composition of the eyes, we see things a bit differently. Humans' intelligence is higher, and our moods are more varied. On one hand, we can be more joyful than horses. On the other hand, our wrath is terrible to behold. We can be very kind and very cruel.

Controlling their tempers seems to be impossible for some trainers and difficult for others. Few people can control their tempers without some form of mind training. It's not enough to feel terrible anger while repressing physical action, for there is a mental bond between horse and human. The horse *knows* when the human feels hate and anger.

We hear about wife beaters, child beaters, and horse beaters. In such situations there's one main point to be considered: the *stronger* is beating the *weaker.* The worst of these fellows wouldn't tackle Mohammed Ali in one of his worst fits of anger, for he knows he'd get punched out pronto.

If I caught an apprentice beating a horse in training, I'd tell him to get "ol' Dynamite" and knock on him a while. The apprentice would refuse, knowing that the horse would wipe him out. I'd answer that the apprentice's temper is *controllable* and that it's cowardly to pick on and beat a horse that won't fight back.

Sometimes my actions belie my words. An apprentice might see me yell, jerk, and hit a horse. He thinks, "This guy loses his temper and has a mighty short fuse." I try to explain that I haven't lost my temper and that I'm not angry. I must get through to the horse that he's made a mistake. Saying "naughty, naughty" to a horse just won't hack it. When I do yell and swat the horse, he understands that I'm upset with him, and, if the lesson takes, he won't make the mistake again. Yet, he doesn't fear me, for he senses no real anger. I haven't hit him hard enough to hurt him.

One day a lady visited our training establishment on a very bad day. It had been raining for days, and the horses were so steamed up they were trying to take advantage of their riders. We were yelling and banging on the horses until I wondered what the visitor would think of us.

When she was about to leave, she said that she'd been around many training barns and had never before seen horses handled with such compassion.

In times past I haven't been able to discipline a horse at all, for my apprentices would consider my actions license for them to half kill a horse. We would be too busy for explanations. I have tolerated being struck and kicked without reprimanding the horse at all, trying to set an example. This is hard, folks, just plain hard.

Horses have off days. This is especially true of young horses, and it is more apt to happen if the trainer has a tendency to overwork his charges. The colt makes a mistake and is punished too harshly. He starts dreading work and soon may become sulky and barn sour.

I was always around horses, and I had a pretty fair idea of how to start one before I began working at it professionally. A lady friend bought a half-Arab filly and raised her in the back yard. The lady's husband, a huge man, wasn't a horseman, and the filly knew it. She started nipping at him in the barn, and he'd jump away from her. Before long she'd chase him out of the pasture. This was great fun.

The lady asked me if I'd ride the filly a few times to get her started. Since she had no facilities, this had to be done in the pasture. Outside of a little crow-hopping, I had no problem with the filly, and she progressed rapidly.

Once this lady decided to do something, she'd start right out to do it. Giving birth to a baby slowed her up enough that I'd had time to get half a dozen rides on the filly.

One nice day the lady got her English saddle and bridle. Right away she saddled up, stuffed the filly's mouth with bits, and climbed on. The filly took a few steps, spooked at a kid on a bike, and hit a mighty buck jump. The lady was bucked down. When the neighbors tried to rescue the lady, the filly stood by and wouldn't let them get near. A neighbor finally coaxed her away with a bucket of oats. The lady was hospitalized for a couple of weeks.

That lady thought I'd done a poor job of starting that filly. I'd used a hackamore, and the lady didn't care much for that. She sent the filly to a farmer for further training.

That big, overgrown farmer put his son on the filly. She bucked the kid down, and the farmer beat her with a hame strap. The filly wasn't just whacked a few times. She was beaten until she'd placidly walk along. Trouble was, that's all she'd do. The lady sold her to a hack stable, and the filly was too deadheaded for that meat factory to use.

We can see all the mistakes that were made with the filly. She thought she could rule the roost. The husband taught her that. Next, the lady went too fast with her. The filly was doing fine with hackamore and stock saddle. The lady's impatience caused the wreck. She was in no physical shape to ride, and she changed the filly's saddle and bit too suddenly.

At this point, the filly could have been salvaged. It would have been a matter merely of having her training set back a bit. But after the terrible beating the filly took, only a long pasture rest could have returned her to a useful, willing mare.

A sudden, blind rash of temper has ruined many a horse. How many horses have had eyes knocked out and necks broken or pulled down and have actually been killed by men with "uncontrollable" tempers.

Farriers have ruined their share of horses, though the horse owner is generally at fault for not teaching the horse to stand for trimming and shoeing. The farrier's work is hard and dangerous. Most of them get pretty hair-triggered after a few years at it.

Ignorance has ruined many a horse. I saw so many stupid things done to horses at the start of my career that I was shocked. When World War II started, people finally had a little money to spend, and a lot of them bought saddle horses. They knew nothing about horses, and there were few people around who could show them anything.

A few high-ups in a war plant got together and bought some horses. These geldings had been condemned by the cavalry. Most of them had minor faults that were tough to correct. One horse was such a bad head tosser that the bits were usually upside down. He'd function with a tie-down.

Those guys hired me to ride the horses. A couple of old broncs were stiff buckers. I was warned that one skinny nag was a killer, for he'd thrown himself on his rider.

That information didn't make sense. The horse had a nice, big eye and was very friendly. One day the owner was gone, and I saddled the horse. No problem. He was an excellent ride. Why had the horse thrown himself on his owner? In this case, putting two and two together was easy. The man weighed nearly 300 pounds, and the horse was so poor, he probably didn't weigh more than 650 pounds. On top of that, the man didn't know how to get on a horse. He'd simply pulled the horse over on top of himself.

Horses are a big thing in my area. There are plenty of boarding stables. Youngsters pester their folks to buy them horses. Trouble is, many kids get colts rather than seasoned horses. The children know little about horses, and the colts know nothing about being ridden. Ignorance plus ignorance equals trouble.

Rather than buy an expensive saddle, the novice buys (or talks the folks into buying) a cheapie from the local tack store. To them, a saddle's a saddle. They don't know that saddles have different widths, so they cinch that narrow rig on that fat, soft back. If the colt's gentle, he won't be that way long.

Some years ago we kept a filly for a girl who had talked her folks into buying this new "toy" for her. The saddle, of course, was a cheapie. My advice wasn't asked for, so I only observed. The girl was definitely afraid of her horse. She longed a half hour before a ride and rode only at a walk and slow trot in the bronc pen. And she was ashamed to tell her folks that she was afraid of that filly after begging so hard to get her.

One afternoon I noticed that the girl's face was very white and that her hands were shaking a bit. I spoke to her about it, and she admitted that she was afraid to the point that she couldn't even think about what she was doing. I asked her if she'd like me to talk to her parents, and she said yes. In fact, she was relieved to shift the problem onto me.

When her parents came out to see her ride the filly, I had a chance to talk to them both together. I told them about the problem, and they were surprised. They had no idea the girl was afraid. I told them I thought it would be a good idea to put the filly in training with us for a couple of months.

I put an extra-wide saddle on the filly, mounted, and rode away. She humped up a little, but, after finding that her back didn't hurt, worked all right. I had no problem with her at any time, except when I tried a regular Quarter Horse saddle on her. The narrower rig upset her so much that she went over backwards several times. She would need a year or so of riding with the extra-wide rig to become a steady mare.

One day I asked the girl to ride her filly. She did and had no problem, except that she never loosened up and enjoyed herself. Her fear of horses was now a permanent thing. Her parents found a buyer for the filly, and the girl had one less problem to contend with.

In my opinion, anger and ignorance go hand in hand. There are many trainers who seem to hate horses. If the horse makes the slightest mistake, the trainer beats him unmercifully. The horse must *absolutely conform* to the trainer's ideas. If not whipped, the horse might be tied, still saddled and bridled, to a post in the hot sun and left there all day. We read such trainers' words of wisdom in many horse magazines. Many of these people are very successful trainers. *Why?* Are their methods wrong or right?

Let's say a trainer gets lucky and has some winning horses he's showing. He gets popular and then has huge numbers of prospects to choose from. If he says a colt won't make it, the colt is sent home. Why won't a particular colt make it? Because he won't stand for the rigid regime of conforming.

A "trainer" may drag a colt around for a couple hours on a hot walker. Then he saddles and works him. After that, the colt's tied to a post all day. This "teaches him patience."

If someone worked that trainer until he was worn out, then strapped a backpack on him and tied him up in the sun all day, you'd hear him holler for ten miles. When that backpack started to eat up his back, when those flies worked him over, he'd be ready to fight. It'd be hard work doing it to him again.

Some horses take it and go on to be winners. The ones that won't are "no good." The owner may sell them or send them to some other trainer, who'll have his work cut out for him.

This is the day of the trainer-showman. The trainer who shows and *wins* usually has a long waiting list. He may have forty horses in training, but he's personally involved with only a few. The few he shows are the "pick of the litter." The rest? His helpers work them. Some go on to make good horses. Others make mediocre horses. Some are spoiled and sent home as worthless (spoiled is a relative word; it doesn't mean that those horses can't be retrained).

Once upon a time, a Texas trainer wasn't doing much, so he moved east. He owned a pretty fair stallion, and would return to Texas to show him. There were a lot of good stallions in Texas, however, so he didn't do all that much winning. So he castrated the horse.

He then had a superior gelding in the days when there wasn't that many good geldings. He showed the horse at halter and in some working classes had a consistent winner. Since he had an East Coast address, many folks assumed that he was a very superior trainer who could haul to Texas and beat everyone there.

His reputation grew. Before long he had all the horse-training work that he wanted. Quite a few "would-be" trainers became trainers while working for him.

One fellow I know took a colt to this top trainer. He did a bit of reading and found that the trainer had never even seen his colt. He got the colt back fairly well-trained, but he was a bit disappointed at not getting the trainer he had asked for.

I have few faults to find with this particular trainer, for

he did teach his help well. Though I've heard of a few horses they "spoiled," they had a fine batting average.

There are other trainers—"club men"—who started in a similar manner. They teach their help to be club men. What does a club man expect from his horses? A colt should stand tied all day just as if he's an auto with the switch turned off. He should never nicker or pay any sort of attention to other horses. He should stand like a statue, ready for mounting. During the ride he should be willing to learn and never make a mistake. If flies are eating him up, he should ignore them. If the trainer's in a bad mood and kicks him in the belly, he should show no signs of fight or fear but merely stand and look unhappy about getting his belly kicked.

When being shod, he should stand still, neither trying to pull his hoof away nor putting any weight on the shoer.

If he's a stallion, he should never notice a mare while he is being handled or ridden. If the handler wants him to breed a mare, however, he must march right up to her (paying no attention to the whip that's warping him on the legs) and quietly, gently, breed her.

If the club man's horses don't measure up to all of this, they get beaten half to death. I've seen trainers who go to church, teach Sunday school, and let their kids get away with murder expect their horses to turn on and off like light bulbs. They seem to think that a horse isn't like a person, that the horse can't think, and that he doesn't feel pain, thirst, hunger, itching, boredom, and so on. He rules with an iron hand much like the heartless "supermen" who ruled the Nazi concentration camps.

But there're two sides to every coin. Horses can be spoiled by the lack of discipline as well as by cruelty. The trainer can be too permissive. He can let his colts get away with too much, just as parents can let their children get away with too much. This is where experience stands the trainer in good stead.

A child-beater might quote the old saw, "Spare the rod and spoil the child." There's a fine line between discipline and abuse. The undisciplined child loses respect for his parents, while the offspring of child-beaters learn to hate their parents. So it is with horses.

The wise parent will at times be rigid. There are certain rules to be followed, and the child must respect those rules. The parent should, however, put himself in his child's shoes, remember how it was to be a child.

1. Fear. The horse is afraid of objects and won't cross water. Such a fearful horse can, and usually does, have poor eyesight. He can have small eyes and get a poor picture of what he's supposed to be seeing.

The timid rider also plays a part in this. If the horse finds that he can buffalo a timid rider, he may do so. A person who's naturally a bit timid should ride brave horses.

2. Spooks or balks. A fine stallion was purchased by a man who had suffered a broken back from a horse wreck. He was afraid of getting hurt again. When the horse made any sort of refusal, he'd dismount and lead him back to the barn. This made the horse barn sour.

The owner's farm manager would beat the horse when he misbehaved. This confused the horse so much that he learned to balk. The first man spoiled the horse by being *weak,* while the second man spoiled him by being *strong.* Both helped spoil the horse through *ignorance.*

3. Rearing. A colt was hauled to a showman-trainer for reining. After a few months, the colt was spoiled and sent home. He'd rear up, sometimes going over backwards, when asked to stop or roll back. First, the colt wasn't a reining horse prospect. When the stop hurt his mouth and legs, his

tendency was to rear. Second, the trainer and his help rode the colt *one way.* He spoiled because he wouldn't conform to the usual pattern. Third, reining training should have been stopped when rearing tendencies became apparent. The colt could have been trained to be a fine trail or pleasure horse.

4. Rank horse, cinchbinder, bucker. The owner tried to start this colt himself. He saddled the filly in the stall. When he pulled the cinch, she exploded and had the terrorized man trapped in the stall for a couple of hours. After deciding he wasn't a horse trainer, he brought the filly to me.

When I got this one to train, I noticed that she was a hard-bucking horse. If I just turned her out for exercise, she'd buck for a half hour all by herself. Hobbles and side-line made her stand for saddling. Checking her up so she couldn't get her head down eventually cured the bucking, for the noseband would rap her painfully if she tried to get her head down to buck.

5. Spoiling. Lest we forget that horses are "people" . . . A famous old Paso mare was inbred. She had a black colt—a very classy one. As a yearling he grew up with another fine colt. His friend got tangled up in some wire, and we had to call the vet. While the injured colt was being doctored, his black friend came up to observe. The vet lightly whacked the black colt to move him out of the way. From this *slight* rebuff, the colt was terrorized. When anyone entered his stall, he'd rear up and run around on his hind legs. It was months before he behaved normally.

When we started riding this black colt, he showed tendencies to be flighty, bullheaded, and rank. However, he was going all right when we sold him. His unstable condition soon became apparent. He became badly spoiled. His new owner couldn't cope with such behavior, and the horse became well known for his outlaw tendencies.

We must remember that there are goofy horses as well as goofy people. One should look for top disposition when buying a horse.

6. Refusals, such as refusing to enter the show ring. We're riding bred-up horses today that are more high-strung than those of yesteryear. Chouse them around in a game show and they can become downright dangerous. This had always been a problem, but it seems there are a lot more screwballs today. Of course, there are a lot more horses.

Most games on horseback are very rough on horses. Take a horse out on a hot, humid day, run the heck out of him, hurt his mouth for hours, and he'll be reluctant to "play" again. A thousand-pound horse can offer mighty strong resistance in many ways. Running away, rearing, and balking are all ways the horse has to tell us he's had it with games. The same goes for horse-show events. It's just plain, hot, dreary work out there for a horse. If he's had boring, wearying training, he'll resent going into the ring to work. "All work and no play. . . ."

I have written quite a bit about humans and their tempers. I *think* I have mine pretty well under control as far as horses are concerned, but . . .

One morning my wife asked me to look at the washing machine. Now, she should know better, and I should know better. If the matter is plumbing, I can become a raving lunatic in short order. The washing machine seemed OK, but a leak was coming from a washstand next to it.

As I was messing around with the washstand, the pipes suddenly began shooting forth water from a connection. I quickly tried to close the shut-off valve, but it broke. At this point I was about to smash everything with the pipe wrench. I would have brained the Incredible Hulk if he'd walked into the room. I was ready to bite myself.

Before wreaking all the havoc I intended, I did try to

tighten the fixture, and the Lord helped me. The spurting water stopped spurting. I got a cup of coffee, lighted a cigarette, and sat out on the porch until I cooled off.

Now a moron could have bought some new parts and fixed the plumbing, but I decided to hire it done. Otherwise I would put myself into another such situation whereby I'd want to blow up the whole town.

After I calmed down and started typing this chapter, I thought, "Is this how some people feel about their horses?" If so, they'd better "hire a plumber."

# 15. Leading, Loading, and Hauling

SUCH a heading as "Leading, Loading, and Hauling" may seem a bit strange, but there's a reason for it. One Australian trainer-writer claimed that the reason many horses are so hard to load is that they've never been taught to lead. All they've learned is to *follow* a man rather than be led, so they just stop following whenever they feel like it. He says that when a horse learns to walk or trot alongside a man without question, the horse will pop right into a trailer or van when he's asked (or told) to. I believe him.

When we start training baby colts to lead, I try to take the safest path I know. With all the arenas and lots we have here, a colt must lead right from the start. We broke outside broodmares' colts this year and never got one of them excited.

A longe line makes a good lead rope. Using a bowline knot, we tie one end around the colt's barrel at the cinch, then run the line between the colt's legs and up through his halter. When he resists, the pull of this rope keeps him on the ground. If he falls, he'll fall sideways and won't flip over backwards.

The other end has a three-foot loop tied in it. This is the *persuader.* The first end keeps him facing forward. The other end, the *butt rope,* brings him right along. We use this until the colt no longer needs the butt rope. After a month or so we may feel that it's safe to lead him with nothing more than halter and lead rope.

Little colts itch. If we take a little time to scratch their itchy spots, they are easier to catch when we want to bring them in from the pasture.

After the colt is weaned, we usually don't handle him too much unless he's going to be shown as a yearling. If he's not going to be shown at halter, he may forget his early leading lessons.

If he is to be shown at halter, he must lead perfectly, because during part of the class he must trot alongside the person showing him. Let's say a colt has been taught to lead well. How was this done? Perhaps his owner noted that he wouldn't lead well and had a helper follow behind with a buggy whip or longe whip. When the colt tried to fall back or stop, he was tapped with the whip. Since he must do this to perfection, he was drilled at correct leading. Chances are he learned to load in a trailer early.

If help was not available, the showman could have used a buggy whip to reach back and tap the colt on the rump if he didn't lead up correctly. In any event, the colt learned that he had to stay beside the handler, no matter what.

When he wanted to load the colt into a trailer, the show-man would lead the colt to it, let the colt look it over, and then demand that he load as he demanded that he lead.

For such colts loading is no problem. For others, a little time can be taken to teach the colt to load in the same fashion. If you know you have to load the colt, say, a week from Saturday, start teaching him to lead immediately. This is, I'm sure, the best method and one that's easiest on the colt.

Some people try and fail. They might ask the horseman to load the colt for them. The horseman may use a war bridle over the halter. This should be used to get the colt's attention. If the colt tries to pull away from the trailer, the war bridle keeps him in position.

The horseman then uses a buggy whip to *annoy* the colt, not hurt him. He taps the colt on the rump. The colt wrings his tail in annoyance, but the trainer keeps tapping him. With nowhere to go but in, the colt enters the trailer. He's rewarded with a treat, petting, and kind words. After a bit he's backed off the trailer, and the process is repeated until the colt loads well.

Other, but poorer, methods include the use of a butt rope, or two butt ropes that are crossed, or a butt rope used with the buggy whip. Caution: don't hurt the horse with the whip, for you don't want him to dread the trailer.

Horses are individuals. A fine dressage horse was brought here, because he'd developed a habit of stopping and rearing. This was simply a canine-tooth problem. Sawing the canine teeth off solved the problem. But the horse was hell to load.

Sul had demolished a trailer and a paddock fence when they tried to load him at home. It took three days before he gave up. When he was ready to go home, he gave us fits. We all took turns using our favorite methods, to no avail. The owner, who loved her horse, stood by as we applied assorted tortures to him. Nothing worked. He'd rear and lunge away from the trailer, and he'd charge right over a person. And he was seventeen and a half hands high.

I've never heaped so much abuse on a horse before. I felt like Attila the Hun. No whip I had would so much as ripple his hair. I fired my revolver behind him. He didn't flick an ear at it. It was hot. All the people attending the event were worn out. We did all the work, while this danged horse remained cool and unruffled. After being beat on for two hours, he looked freshly groomed. When we had to rest, he'd calmly eat grass.

When I'm truly perplexed with a problem horse, I like to have a cup of coffee and a cigarette or two. I asked the others to wait for me while I had my usual meditation routine.

After finishing the coffee to the dregs and stubbing out the last cigarette, I brought out a stout, poly lariat, and tied it around the horse's cinch area, and ran it through the halter. I took this to the trailer's centerpost and made several turns around the post where it came out of the floor. This ensured that he wouldn't bend or break the post.

I asked the others to tie a rope to each of his four legs. One person would pull a leg forward, then another would pull a leg, and another, and another. I pulled my rope tight and kept it that way. He couldn't rear up very much, and when he tried, he was pulled forward and down. He couldn't turn away. He knew we had him, so he lay down.

There were four ladies present. Three out of four voted to shoot him, but I nixed it. We brought up a hose and watered him well. He liked it, except on the head. This got him up. He tested all the ropes again, and realizing there was no way out, he calmly walked into the trailer and stood. All of us five horse folks were hot, pooped, drained, and disgusted, for we really felt that the horse had won. This horse had been hauled when he was a yearling and never even loaded again until time for his trip to me. I've been told he loads well now.

Horses load well in trailers with no ramp but hesitate to step down out of the trailer until they're seasoned travelers. The trailer with the back-door ramp is the one I favor.

The small, cheap, two-horse, side-by-side trailers with a solid divider are abominations. Never, never haul two horses in such a rig. When you haul one, remove the divider and let him stand at an angle. The new trailers that have angled stalls are pretty nice.

The horse wants to spread his legs wide for stability. When his hooves hit the solid walls, he panics and fights. He may lunge and get his front hooves in the manger. He may break the trailer, turn around, tear the door down, and jump out.

A wider, two-horse, side-by-side with a bar for a partition works better. The horse can spread his legs and brace himself. The in-line trailers are better still. The large trailers built for hunters are fine, for they give most horses ample room.

Large stock trailers are even better. You can turn a horse loose in the front half and turn a horse loose in the back half. You guessed it. I like a four-horse stock trailer for two horses. They can turn around and haul anyway they want to.

If you haul in a small trailer, you need to be very careful about your driving. In a stock trailer it's not as important, but taking as much care as possible is the thing to do. Start slowly and stop slowly. Turn the wheel a little before turning to tell the passengers that you'll soon make a turn.

I prefer a van. The small, four-horse vans are wonderful if you can afford them. You can build your own on a one-ton or larger chassis. If you get there, your horses get there. There may be problems, however.

A friend and I were going to a rodeo at Niagara Falls, New York. My rope horse was in the back end of the truck. My friend and I were getting a little tired and sleepy, so we stopped to fill the thermos with coffee.

On the road again my friend poured a cup of boiling-hot brew into my cup and handed it to me. We were in bumper-to-bumper traffic. The driver ahead of us slammed on his brakes and pulled into a motel parking lot. I slammed on the brakes, and the hot coffee spilled onto my lap.

Folks, I may have been screaming my head off, but I kept the truck on the road and drove on. Moral? You bet. Don't do that.

Hauling my two-year-old stallion Tengo Tivio and a three-year-old filly, Miss Wonaway, to Harrisburg, Pennsylvania, I had to go through a little town on the way to the Pennsylvania Turnpike. I was driving slowly when a man suddenly pulled out in front of me. I stood on the brakes and whipped the wheel left. Just missed him. Crash! The horses had been stood on their heads.

I looked through the window and noted that the horses were all right, so we moved on. I made it to the turnpike and was going up through the gears when a car shot around us, skidded, and spun out right in front of the van. Cripes! I had to stand on the brakes again. As it was, the van just touched his car. He got going and gunned away from us. I checked the horses. Tengo was OK, but Missy was nervous. I decided the best thing to do was drive on.

When we got to Harrisburg, I *eased* up to a light. Crash! Missy blew up, set back, broke her halter, broke down the butt bar, reached forward with a hind hoof, and kicked the tack trunk apart. It was in the center stall. She skinned herself up (before the halter class) but had no permanent injuries.

That was a long time ago. Traffic's ten times worse now. Anyone who shows much can tell better tales than this. It's a wonder that show folk can even get their horses to come near a show rig.

# 16. The Hard-to-Mount Horse

A horse that won't stand still while being mounted is both irritating and dangerous. A Paso stallion we have in now is hard to mount. He has to be cheeked. This does nothing to teach a horse to stand. Pasos, like some Arabians, are often nervy, quick horses. They're easy to spoil. Stick a sharp boot toe into the side of such a horse, twist it around as you mount, and he'll be hard to get on next time. They always remember. We used to have mounting sessions about this. I'd loosely cinch up a gentle horse, or not even secure the cinch. Then I'd place my hand under the apprentice's knee and tell him that I didn't want to feel pressure on my hand. He'd have to mount without pulling the saddle and without sticking the horse with toe or knee.

How do you learn how to do this? I'd place my hand under a rider's foot and tell him to dismount. I didn't want him to hurt my hand. He could get down in one quick, fluid motion, putting no pressure on my hand. To mount? Do just the opposite. Spring up, keeping close to the horse and putting only a little, even pressure on the stirrup. When above the horse, bear down on the horn with your hand, your weight on your hand. Ease down. In this way you can mount without pulling the saddle or sticking the horse.

But how do you train a horse who just won't stand? Having someone hold the horse helps, but you might not always have help available. Altonero, a big Paso gelding, was bad to get on, and he had seriously injured a person while being mounted. He spun, whirled, reared, and hit the rider in the face with his head. When he became truly dangerous to mount, he was sent to me for training.

My wife, who is not very tall, uses a mounting block. I led Altonero to her mounting block and fooled around with him until I got him to stand. Then I had to work to get him to stand while I was standing on the mounting block. After something like ten minutes, he stood well enough for me to mount. We went for a long ride.

Next day he went right up to the block and stood there. The block was placed about three feet out from a tall fence. I climbed up on the block, stepped across him, and we went for a long calm pleasant ride.

I always used the mounting block with this horse. One windy day my hat blew off when we were far out in the pasture. I got off, retrieved my hat, and mounted Altonero. He stood still as a statue. After a month or so of *not* being annoyed by clumsy mounting, he stood well.

If the horse is trained well enough to be ridden outside, a wing can be built alongside a good fence (or building). Steps can be incorporated into this wing. The wings keep him from swinging this way or that. After mounting, give him a reward, a bite of something he likes. Soon he'll learn to stand and wait for this reward.

A few posts and a little lumber don't cost much, and the rewards are great. It may not seem very macho to use a mounting block, but it's good horse training.

Some trainers might say that you'll *always* have to use a mounting block and *always* have to reward the horse. This just isn't so.

The modern horse trainer in this country seldom uses a blindfold. I saw them in wide use in Colombia and learned that they're in wide use all over South America. Horse trainers there just build a blindfold (*tapa ojos,* or "eye cover") onto a bridle or *jáquima* and use it constantly. We had to

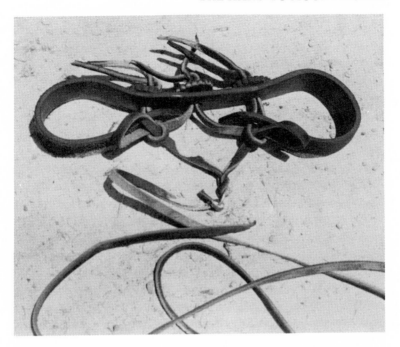

Breakaway hobbles.

train some of these horses to stand for mounting *without* the customary blindfold, and it was wild. They'd snort, arch into a semi-circle, tremble, and squat. They had to be cheeked. To cheek a horse, the rider grasps the headstall or the fiador of the hackamore, pulls the horse to him, mounts quickly, and lets go the hold.

A hobble that the rider can pull free from the saddle is a pretty fair piece of equipment. We used such hobbles on a buzzy colt for months, and he gradually learned to stand for mounting. He had me about whipped, for I'd run out of methods and decided to try the hobbles as a last resort. They went with the colt when he left here, just in case he gave his owner trouble.

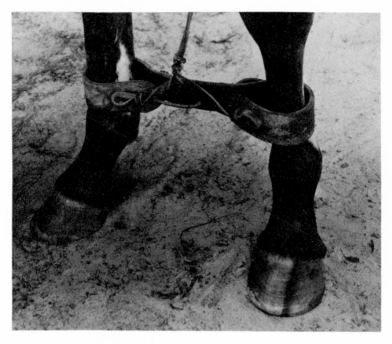

Breakaway hobbles in use.

To use them, you should have the horse well-trained to regular hobbles and sideline. A colt may learn to run on front hobbles, so I believe that a sideline should always be used with the front-leg hobbles at first. When the colt knows better than to run on hobbles, a rig such as the breakaway hobble can be used.

Some trainers consider mounting a hobbled horse a very dangerous thing to do. Other trainers do this as a matter of course. I'm middle-of-the-road on this. You need to have enough experience to be able to make an educated guess as to whether or not it's safe to mount this particular hobbled horse. The expression of the eyes, mouth, and ears tell a lot. Watch out for the deadpan horse who shows no expression.

206

I first saw this hobble illustrated in Bruce Grant's book *How to Make Cowboy Horse Gear.* Later I saw a drawing by Randy Steffen of the same thing. Steffen said that he saw an Indian horsebreaker using it.

The Paso we're currently working gets up-tight for first mounting. Getting him to stand at the mounting block took about five minutes the first time we tried it. After being ridden a bit, he'll stand for regular mounting and dismounting.

I often write about the *Jeffery Method of Horse Handling,* in which the author advocates the use of a rope around the horse's neck that is operated with quick pulls and releases. This takes the horse's mind off misbehaving, and we keep a short rope on hand for this purpose. This works on some hard-to-mount horses.

# 17. The Bucking Horse

I was once breaking horses with a man whom I considered to be very good. One day I noticed a colt buck with him, and to my surprise he let out a yell and cowboyed that bucking colt. He never tried to pull him up but rode that colt with his hackamore reins loose.

That evening we talked to the colt's owner, an old cowman. He was perturbed when he heard that his colt bucked and asked my friend why he had allowed the colt to pitch. My friend, who was a talker as well as a doer, told him that the colt caught him off-guard, but he had turned him into a fence and made him stop. He assured the cowman that the colt wouldn't be allowed to buck in the future.

Sure enough, the colt didn't buck again, but it wasn't because his rider didn't give him the opportunity. He had a free head and open spaces. The colt just stopped bucking.

Since then, I have heard of many horsemen who say they never allow their horses to buck. I have seen strange rigs to hold a horse's head up, and I have heard riders tell of spinning the horse to keep him from bucking.

I once had many green range colts to break. This was a monotonous job, since the colts weren't rank and didn't need to be finished to perfection. They were range colts, though, and once in a while one of them would pitch a little. I was a little bronco, too, and had a slight interest in riding the rough ones, so I didn't object at all. I had no one around to tell me not to allow those colts to buck, so

David Baggett fanning a big bronc with his hat.

when one did hop a little, it was a welcome relief from boredom.

I never went after one of those colts too hard when he bucked. I didn't want to scare the buck out. I was too much horseman to encourage it. The trouble was that after a few rides, none of those colts wanted to buck anymore. It seemed as if they didn't have a thing to become fighty about. I didn't yank or beat them, and I also didn't ride around holding up their heads. They all gentled out very nicely.

We had a stud on that outfit who was quite a fighter. He was mean to handle on the ground and could buck pretty fair, and he would do so at unexpected times and places. No

Attorney Jack Peeples riding Spike.

one was anxious to use him, because you never could tell when he would make you "meet your shadow."

This stud struck me once and got a whipping for it. I didn't really go after him, but just spanked him carelessly with my rope. When he got the idea that I wasn't afraid of him, his attitude toward me changed, and he was a good one as far as I was concerned. As long as I handled him recklessly, he gave me no trouble. I liked him, because he was a fearless horse, very sure-footed, fast, and tough.

210

Jack Peeples riding Spike.

Others fared no better with him than they had before I started riding him. They would be choking the horn to stay with him, while I could throw my rig on him and go to work cattle or rope. They were too careful, and he knew they were afraid of him.

I have never seen a colt or spoiled horse come out of the bucking habit successfully with the "not allowing" deal. If he had the buck in him, no matter how careful the rider, sooner or later he would catch the rider unaware and buck, often with disastrous results.

Today's horses are started younger and fed better than they were before 1950. They're apt to buck because they feel good, or because the saddle doesn't fit right. The young horse has a lot of baby fat on his back. If the saddle digs in and causes him pain, he'll probably buck to get rid of it. The colt who bucks when asked to canter, but doesn't buck at a walk or trot is probably being pinched.

To test this, try an extremely wide saddle on him. If he doesn't buck, you have your answer. After this baby fat wears off, he'll probably go all right in a narrower saddle.

On a hot day, put a Kodel polyester pad on under the saddle. These pads are called "cool back," because a horse really sweats when wearing one. The moisture is supposed to keep his back cool. If there's a pressure point where the saddle is pinching him, that point will be dry. Keep trying saddles on him until his whole back is wet.

Another place that bothers colts is the point where the latigo crosses the cinch ring. It makes a definite lump. The more wraps of the latigo you use, the heavier the lump is. It helps to use a cinch cover for this condition, but a cinch chafe offers better protection. Most big saddleries stock them. We make a simple variety that most horsemen could make themselves.

Spurs often cause bucking. The colt spooks at something

and jumps. The rider is wearing spurs. He grips tight with his legs, and the spurs grab the colt. The colt bucks the rider down.

I've cured a few horses of bucking by whipping them on the nose, but it doesn't always work. A hard double will often do more. A man once bugged me to take his stud to train. This horse had bad points instead of good ones. He had to be ridable so the man could sell him. Of course he gave me the ol' pizazz about the horse being untrained rather than spoiled. I later found out that his horse had bucked off everyone his owner talked into trying him.

The horse moved off all right until I asked him to lope. He then sank his head, bawled, and bucked around the pen. I got a quirt and managed to ride while whipping him on the nose, as Ed Connell suggested. The horse just got his head as far out of the way as he could while bucking and bawling like a rutting bull.

Years before, I had bought a Severe Brothers hackamore that was one inch in diameter and very stiff. I put that on the bronc. When he dropped his head, I fed him slack rein and then came up with all the power I had. This peeled quite a bit of hide off his jaw. I tried him again. When he dropped his head, I got him on the other side. He decided he had enough of bucking. I went ahead with him, which pleased and dumbfounded his owner.

I've trained a few horses that seemed to be born to buck. One such was a filly who almost got her owner. He'd decided to break her himself and saddled her in her stall. When he pulled the cinch snug, she blew up. He cowered in a corner for a couple of hours. Every time he'd move at all, she'd blow up and fire.

This man fed me the same old diluted prune juice about the filly being unspoiled. When he read my contract, he changed his tune. I have a nonliability clause that states the

Ken Serco's first ride on a born-to-buck filly. She's looking back at him, ready to explode.

owner isn't liable if my apprentices or I get hurt by the owner's horse *unless* the horse has been misrepresented—spoiled rather than untrained, for instance.

We hobbled and sidelined the filly. When she was familiar with the hoof restraints, we saddled her and slipped a hackamore on her head. She was checked up enough that the noseband would give her a good rap if she dropped her head to buck. She did buck and kept it up a long time. After a couple of weeks, she'd run around without bucking.

214

Ken bucking down. A really hard fall.

We trained her to drive in longe lines. She was still checked up. Her first driving session consisted of some very wild lurching, but she soon settled down.

Ken Serco gave her her first ride. All went well for a while but something spooked her. She fired and bucked him down hard. But that was the end of it. She never bucked again while being ridden. After each ride, she'd buck for her play.

One of the few times we sent one home was for bucking. A local veterinarian had a Thoroughbred gelding that was bad news. He'd injured the vet several times before the vet sent him here. The horse was small-eyed, with a narrow forehead.

My apprentice at the time was Australian Ranald Cameron. All the ground work went well, but when the gelding was ridden for the first time, he bucked Ranald down six times. The horse went six feet in the air every jump. At the apex of his jump, he'd kick straight up, and this is what got Ranald. Ranald couldn't whip his legs foreward fast enough to stay aboard.

This horse bucked in such a classy fashion, I advised the owner to sell him to a rodeo company. He didn't do this but did send the horse to a man who had a little rodeo school. The horse kept bucking people down but lost his former reliability. Eventually he wrecked his owner, and the horse was sold to a person who thought he'd eventually work out of it.

Ranald could double the horse and stop his bucking, but when he did so, the horse would sulk or balk. I thought the horse was potentially very dangerous and would have liked to see him go to a rodeo producer who could use a horse with a real flair for fancy bucking.

# 18. Kickers and Strikers

NOT long ago I read an article by a well-known horse trainer who advised that a kicking horse could be cured by tying a rope from the hackamore, through the stirrup, to the offensive hoof. When the horse kicks, he punishes his nose. The author failed to mention what the results can sometimes be when such a rig is used, for if a horse kicks with much force, he may severely injure his nose. This damage could cause a permanent, unsightly limp and the ruination of a light-nosed hackamore horse. If he really turns loose, he could break his nose. I once saw a colt throw a whingy in such a rig. The nose cracked and infection set in. After much treatment, this fine-headed horse ended up with a heavy, thick, unsightly "camel" nose.

Such treatment might be warranted for a cheap, vicious horse, but there are other, safer ways. In other words, this is not the treatment for kicking horses. The best rig for a kicking horse, however, is the scotch hobble. There are many ways to scotch a horse. Some people advocate attaching a rope to a strap buckled around the pastern. Swell, I say, but if the horse kicks, how are you going to buckle on the strap?

Here's my method: Take fifteen or twenty feet of soft-twist cotton rope, about an inch in diameter. Tie a loop around the horse's neck (bowline knot) with one end. Drop the rope in a U in front of the leg you want to tie up. Lead the horse up until he steps into the U. Draw up the leg and tie the rope through the loop tied around the horse's neck.

The rope should come up, over, and down through the loop instead of up and under. This is much easier to hold if the horse kicks.

Now we have the hoof drawn up, not quite as high as we finally want it. We then take hold of the hoof, pull it up a little, and bend the rope once around the pastern. This prevents a burn as well as making more certain that the horse doesn't kick loose, since he can still kick forward a little.

Some time ago, I devised a hobble rig that works well for starting colts and is very good when handling a kicking horse. When a scotch-hobbled horse kicks, he punishes himself, and the scotch hobble is a good cure. The hobble-sideline rig prevents kicking, is a top breeding hobble when used with double sidelines, and can even be used as a casting rig. A horseshoer can use this rig and free one of the horse's legs at a time, with the other three legs still secured.

The advantage of my hobble-sideline rig is that the hardware doesn't put any twist or strain on the leather hobbles. If the hobbles are used a lot, they'll hold up better.

When a horse is hobbled and sidelined, all he has left to fight with are his teeth. If you slip a wire noseband under his halter, about all he can do is fall on you. He has no way to strike or kick. I've reformed bad kickers and strikers in five minutes. Simply hobble and sideline such a horse and do whatever it is that provokes his kicking or striking. He may try, but he'll fall. If so, the sideline ropes can be shortened and he probably can't get up. Of course, you can go ahead and tie him down once he throws himself.

One horse with a striking problem and a wide reputation for being vicious was hauled here. He'd struck his lady owner in the chest and cracked some of her bones. I was first choice, and the killers were the second.

I hobbled and sidelined the horse. Then I lightly slapped him on the chest. He tried to strike but fell. When he got up, I slapped his chest again. Nothing. I took the foot restraints off and slapped his chest. Nothing.

The lady visited me. I hobbled and sidelined her horse. Then I got a phone call, and talked for ten minutes. The horse stood calmly all the while. I saddled the horse in a careless fashion and gave him a ride. No problems. She was amazed.

While giving spring shots, I was twitching horses and holding the twitch while the veterinarian gave the shots. All went well until we came to Lisana, a three-year-old Paso filly. I applied the twitch. The vet popped the needle into her neck, and suddenly I was lying in the manger on the other side of the stall. She'd struck me in the chest with both front feet, and I'd never seen it coming. My chest must be pretty tough, for it didn't hurt me very much. I could continue.

There's nothing much to say in favor of the twitch. It can give you a false sense of security. Trust it, and you'll get hurt if you handle horses long enough. In Lisana's case, I went to the tack room and found a blindfold, which I slipped over her head. With blindfold in place, Lisana stood quietly for her shots.

OK. Your horse kicks or strikes. How can you get the foot restraints on him? Use a blindfold. Horse hard to saddle? Blindfold him. The blindfold is used universally in South America. I watched Colombians load pack mules. They'd drop a blindfold on the mule's head, and the animal would stand there quietly while he was being loaded.

When Colombians break colts, they use a headstall with a large blindfold-browband attached to it, called a *tapa ojos* (the Peruvians want their Pasos to carry a flat tail, so they use *tapa colas* ["tail covers"] on them). When a Colombian saddles a *potro* ("colt"), he'll slip the *tapa ojos* down over the colt's eyes, bring up the saddle, put it on, tie his *jáquima*

219

*Tapa ojos.*

*reindas* ("hackamore reins") to suit him, step on the colt, lean forward, and push up the *tapa ojos.*

When I make a blindfold, I use a twenty-four-inch-square piece of material such as you find in a cheap saddle blanket. I cut a slit about seven inches long in the center. This allows the blindfold to be dropped over the ears. At the bottom of the blindfold I sew a loop on one side and a thong on the other. This gives me something to tie it down with.

Some Colombians don't train their colts to stand for bridling and saddling without blinds. This is a mess if you happen to get an older horse, for they're hard to retrain.

Whips can be used to correct kicking and striking. I hate to write about them, for many people use them to the extreme. When a confirmed older kicker takes a swipe at you, however, a sharp cut with a whip will usually make him think twice before doing it again.

I think I should interject a word or two about kicking. Only those who have handled wild or semiwild horses know how accurately horses kick and how hard they can kick. When a colt is raised fairly close to humans, he knows he shouldn't kick them. He kicks either as a mild warning or because he's been startled.

In the case of his warning and kicking you, he knows how much force to use without really hurting you. When startled, he may not be accurate, but he may use great force. An acquaintance of mine was permanently crippled when he walked up behind a gentle horse who was half asleep and slapped him on the rump. The horse broke both his hips.

One cold winter day in 1962 I was leading a strong two-year-old stud back to his stall. Suddenly a barn door blew shut. This startled the colt, who jumped forward and lashed back. A hoof hit me in the large muscle of my leg with so much force that I flew twenty feet through the air. He kicked me clear across a road.

He didn't break my leg. I could still limp around, and I managed to catch him. After putting him up, I told the hired hand that I was hurt and had to get to my house pronto.

I iced that leg for three days and then went to liniment. My body from navel to foot was solid purple. After limping around so much my lower back went out, I went to a doctor. He said, "My God! You're a damned fool. A blood clot could have broken loose and killed you." I told him I thought that could have happened if I had gone to a doctor. To this day, if I stand on concrete or hard ground, that part of my right leg goes numb, for the colt destroyed a lot of small blood vessels and probably messed up some nerves.

If you want to see what great control an equine has when it kicks, watch a bunch of broodmares with small colts. Those mares have marvelous patience, for they allow their offspring a lot of mischief *before* they reprimand them. A colt may jump all over his mother's head, strike her repeatedly, kick her, and so on. When she's finally had enough, she'll kick him hard, but I've never seen a mare damage her colt.

When I'm working around horses, I'm whistling, singing, or jabbering away at them constantly. The old-time horsemen were talkers when around horses. This calms the horse, but it also lets the horse know you're there, that you're his friend and nothing to be kicked.

I try to get my apprentices to keep up a chatter when they're working with colts. They do pretty fair, but in stressful moments, such as when they're easing onto a colt for the first time, they invariably shut up. Now, when the colt's used to hearing people jabber all the time and suddenly they're silent, he gets uneasy and becomes very tense. Why have they shut up? It's because humans, just like horses, can really concentrate on only one thing at a time. When they devote all their attention to getting on a colt the first time, other thoughts can't come to them, *unless they talk so much it's automatic.*

This is why the war bridle and the Jeffery method (control rope) are fine training aids when properly used. The horse thinks about the sensation when a war bridle or Jeffery rope is jerked and can't continue to concentrate on kicking or striking. It works. Use it.

Some horses want to kick other horses when they are being ridden. This is a very dangerous situation, and I get a lot of phone calls and letters about it. For all *normal* purposes, you punish (whip) your horse if he tries to kick another horse. Cranky mares are prone to kick. You can't correct insanity with a whip.

Many mares have cystic ovaries. A mare may kick, scream, rear, and urinate if she's cystic. She'll act like she wants to be bred but will kick a stallion while "horsing." However, her urine will be clear. A bred mare may act like this when teased by a stallion.

One day we found in the pasture a filly with a sliver of wood in her hock, so we brought her to the barn. When I started to examine her hock, she kicked, screamed, and urinated all over me. I knew she was cystic.

A few years ago a nice lady brought a Texas mare to me for reformation. The mare had thrown her into a tree, nearly breaking the lady's back. This mare, Broomtail, had always been bad news. As a two-year-old, she'd been sent to a trainer. When he tried to ride her, she bucked up onto a fence and couldn't get down. She had to be removed with a crane. So, in addition to all her other problems, she was terribly afraid of fences.

When we started handling her, I immediately knew she was cystic. Veterinary palpation was next. The vet said her left ovary was the size of a grapefruit, rough as an Osage orange, and had five follicles on it. Her right ovary was shrunken and useless. We tried chorionic gonadotrophin on her three times. Nothing. We tried progesterone on her twice. No help.

In the meantime, the men were riding her. This could be done, but we were getting nowhere. One day, as her rider was dismounting, she screamed, reared, and urinated. When he tried to remove the saddle, she reared and struck at him. While he held her, I managed to rope her, one ear in and one ear out of the loop. By jerking the rope, I managed to hold her attention while he unsaddled her. About this time, Dr. Grady Young, a veterinarian long used to the unusual, had started using hair analysis and mineral supplements with success. He told me about it. I called the laboratory and talked to their public relations man. We made a deal. I got a free hair analysis and some minerals in exchange for writing some articles. We would do a continuing study on various horses. I worked with them for two years.

Broomtail was one of the first horses we analyzed. Her manganese percentage was something like 6.8 mg (2 mg is normal). I talked to their top expert about this. I learned that animals metabolize their food differently, or else they are being fed poor or incomplete rations. When a female has such a high manganese content, the membrane around the ovaries becomes very thick and tough. If the condition can be normalized by supplementing corrective minerals, the situation will straighten out.

Calcium depresses manganese. When we added the prescribed amount of chelated calcium to Broomtail's grain, she became more docile and had no more insane fits.

After Broomtail had received mineral supplementation for a month and a half, her owner called and said that she could take a couple of days off from work and would like to pick up her mare. I had clipped more hair and sent it in for analysis but didn't have the results back yet. I called Albion Laboratories. The tests were complete, and Broomtail's magnesium percentage was down to 3.4 mg. We had the vet come out to examine her again. His eyes widened as he exclaimed, "Both ovaries are normal and functioning." Broomtail's owner sent in more hair for analysis a few months later. The results were normal.

Recently a local plantation owner asked me about two cystic mares she had. We ordered calcium and gave it to both mares. Both cleared up in a short time.

We've used mineral supplements on many horses over the years with great success. The conditions we've corrected include anemia brought on by worms, stress, and poor care at home; arthritis; bone spurs and/or splints; nervousness; wood chewing; and, of course, cystic ovaries.

Many veterinarians oppose hair analysis and mineral supplements because either they had no such training in college or they consider the hair analysis difficult to read and understand. All they need to do is call Albion's toll-free number (see the end of this chapter) for help in reading the results.

What we're after is a mineral balance. If the horse's analysis shows an imbalance, the computer immediately prints out what minerals are needed to correct the balance. As for being hard to read, the reports are clear to the analyst who does a little detective work. We need to know what happens when a specific condition is present.

For instance, a horse seems to have pain when he is working, but no one has been able to pinpoint the painful area. A hair analysis is taken, and it reads high in calcium. For this we would give calcium, magnesium (to move calcium deposits), and, probably, iron and copper. We find that nearly all horses are low in copper. Iron must have copper to work properly.

We add these minerals to the grain, and in a few days

we see improvement. In a week or so the horse seems to work with no pain. After a couple of months, we send in more hair for analysis. We find that the horse now reads a little low in calcium. How can this be? We've fed calcium daily, and yet the horse reads low.

The first analysis showed that the horse's body was not using calcium properly. The calcium was "sticking" in specific places, building up and causing pain. It also "stuck" in the hair, so the reading showed a high calcium content. Picture this process as a series of rivers and lakes. The rivers dry up, but the lakes contain still water (not moving). The lakes are reservoirs. Bone and tissue need the calcium, but it is lacking in specific places. The added calcium and magnesium empty out the reservoirs. The rivers flow again, and we have moving water. The stored calcium, which has been causing the pain, moves and is utilized in bone and tissue.

Someone must put two and two together, not just read the results and call them stupid or unscientific. As a trainer, I always consider new possibilities as well as standard methods.

Ask:

Albion Laboratories, Inc.
P.O. Box 750
Clearfield, Utah 84015
Telephone: 800-453-2406

# 19. Barn-Sour and Runaway Horses

IF a horse is whipped, manhandled, or overworked; has pain under saddle; or suffers other such bad treatment, he may become barn sour. He may love another horse and do almost anything to get back to him. At any rate, all he can think about is getting back to the barn.

The barn means comfort, no work, food, water, equine companionship, and temporary freedom from man. No wonder a horse loves it so.

A sorrel gelding, Scuba Too, was brought here for retraining. This horse had been raced and then put to barrel racing with no real training as a foundation. He'd been abused. His present owner told me that he'd seen Scuba being severely whipped at a show by a former owner. He told the owner that he'd lend him his gun so he could kill the horse quickly rather than wear himself out beating him to death.

A horse that's been severely whipped will usually be resentful and will have developed a dislike for man. We wanted this horse to like us, so we started handing out treats. We found that Scuba liked carrots, so those were what we used. (I often get peculiar looks when I go to the grocery store, because I may pick up six bunches of carrots and a couple of gallons of apple-cider vinegar).

Scuba was saddled and ridden in the breaking pen. He kicked up a lot, fought his head, gnashed his teeth, and wanted to run wide open. When Wayne Frey, his rider, stopped Scuba and offered him a piece of carrot, the horse dropped it and became *furious.* He snapped his teeth and pawed the ground like a top boxer jabbing an opponent.

The horse had been raced in a snaffle bit, and barrel-raced in a mechanical hackamore. We had to use something different.

When I was a kid, I had a job on a Standardbred track. The boss had an old trotter he wanted to retire from racing and sell as a saddle horse (he was too tight to just retire the horse). He asked me to see if I could train him to ride.

Wow! That old horse could trot fast, but he wouldn't canter at all. When I'd get him stopped, I would feel as if I'd been riding a jackhammer. And I was getting nowhere.

One night I slipped into a bar to have a couple beers with some friends. After a while, a man walked over to our booth and asked if I was the kid who'd been riding ol' Peter Skilo. I told him I was that very kid.

He said the horse should be ridden with something on his head that he'd never worn before, and he asked if I knew what a hackamore was. I did know, and thanked him for the information.

Well, this sounded pretty dumb to me, but I was ready to try anything. I rigged a rope noseband on the old horse and gave it a try. After a few false starts, ol' Pete hit a canter and seemed to enjoy it. He started working in fine fashion.

A week or so later the boss found a young couple who wanted the horse for driving. We hooked Peter to a jog cart so they could give him a try. The boss climbed onto the seat, started the horse, and immediately ol' Pete broke out into a nice, slow canter.

A friend of mine, Pete Madison, is an 80-year-old cowboy, trainer, and philosopher who works in Los Angeles. A few years ago Pete had a similar problem and asked me about it. I told him about using the hackamore. I guess Pete thought I was handing out silly advice, but he tried it and it worked.

Following my own advice, I told Wayne to try Scuba in a hackamore. Wayne was a little leery about this, but he did it. At least Scuba could take a piece of carrot without dropping it and losing his temper. We seldom see horses actually display bad temper, but Scuba would plainly tell us how he felt.

Scuba was going fairly well in the breaking pen, and he would bend his neck enough to be controlled in the arena—and *controlled* was all. He'd stick (semi-balk) going from the direction of the barn and wanted to run full blast back to it. We had to break this barn-sour pattern.

During saddling, Scuba would cow-kick, but he wouldn't actually try to hit his rider. I told Wayne to ignore that stuff temporarily. For control during saddling, we used the Jeffery rope. Wayne would jerk and release it when Scuba acted up.

Wayne had the hard task of staying in the pasture with Scuba until he could walk the horse back to the barn on a loose rein. He carried a bunch of carrots. Riding to the back pasture, Wayne got off and tried to graze the horse. But it was winter. The grass had died, and Scuba didn't care for it. This works well when the grass is good, for the barn-sour horse is allowed grass only far out in the pasture, never close to the barn. This shows the horse that things are very nice away from the barn and not so hot back home.

We went the carrot route. Before a ride, Wayne would split a lot of carrots down the middle and then cut them into bite-sized pieces. This preparation would prevent the excited horse from choking on a whole, round piece of carrot.

After riding in the pasture (usually a wide-open, circular run, with Wayne doing his best to pull and release the hackamore reins), Wayne would dismount, unsaddle, and feed Scuba all those carrots. But when he'd saddle up and try to ride Scuba home at a walk, the fight would start all over again. That first pasture ride was a dilly. But we were making

229

progress. When Wayne managed to bring Scuba back cool rather than dripping sweat, we knew we were on the right track.

I've reformed many horses that wanted to run back to the barn. You can't hold them in. You have to circle them with a low, wide, loose rein. For this you use a hackamore or a colt bit. You need a bit guard with the colt bit so that you don't pull the bit rings into the horse's mouth.

One of the worst ones I reformed was Wilda Boy. He'd been raced and cowboyed by kids who ran him full blast back to the barn.

Wilda Boy would walk away from the barn, but as soon as he turned toward it, he'd squat, leap, and do frog jumps. If he got some slack in the reins, he'd run wide open to his stall.

One day I had enough. I saddled Wilda Boy and rode him to the far end of the largest arena we had. He was wearing a colt bit and bit guard. When we turned toward the barn, he started his usual stuff, but I directed him into a circle by pulling and releasing the rein. I sat back in the saddle so I wouldn't encourage him to run by leaning forward. I would stay out there all day if I had to.

Without pain from a curb bit, the horse will soon realize that the stupid rider is preventing him from running back to the barn. He sees that he's getting no closer to the barn and is just charging around for no reason at all. The run becomes a lope, then a canter, trot, and, finally, a walk. When the horse walks on a loose rein, he's allowed to head toward the barn.

The horse then decides to get to the barn faster, so he picks up speed. But the crazy person on his back again makes him circle. No use getting all hot and sweaty. Back to the walk. He's again allowed to walk toward the barn.

With Wilda Boy, the loose-rein walk to the barn took an hour or so. He went on to become a good cow horse.

All of this worked with Scuba Too, but it took days, weeks, rather than an hour, since he'd had no previous training. Our biggest problem was conquered. You could take Scuba out on a trail ride and *walk* him back to the barn. He was still rewarded with carrots in the pasture.

Scuba kicked up during arena work. He'd lay his ears back, gnash his teeth, and kick at the sky. I told Wayne to keep his legs way off the horse, because I realized that Scuba had been spurred *HARD* somewhere down the road. This worked, but the horse must eventually learn to respond to the legs if you want to do much with him.

Next I told Wayne to hit him with the flat of his hand and yell loudly when Scuba kicked. This was taking quite a chance, for we'd just gotten Scuba over the barn-sour bit. But a horse will put up with a lot from a person if that person doesn't lose his temper and does reward the horse for good work. This worked. Scuba gradually stopped kicking and allowed Wayne to use a little leg pressure.

Problems kept cropping up. Scuba developed lumps on his back, in the saddle-blanket area. We usually use Cool Back pads. Before long there were about twenty hard lumps on his back. After veterinary consultation, we decided the lumps were caused by an allergic reaction. Scuba was given an anti-histamine and switched to Navajo-type blankets. The lumps gradually went down. Finally, most of Scuba's problems were diminished or gone. The owners consented to leave him another month to give us a chance to set good behavioral patterns.

Scuba didn't want to load to go home. I suggested the trailer was too small for him. His owners agreed, but it was all they had at the moment. The owner's wife cut a little switch, swished it through the air, and said "Scuba, you ol' rascal, get on the trailer," and he did.

On the way home, he tore up the trailer. When they unloaded him, he rope-burned the owner's wife, jumped a ditch, and landed on the owner's foot.

Scuba Too has since gentled down and is truly loved by the whole family. Now that he's had some training, he responds to affection, and he has been barrel-raced with no adverse reaction. He's ridden daily and loves it.

# 20. The Spooking, Shying Horse— The Timid Horse

THE owner rode his horse a long way without checking the cinch. The horse shied and jumped sideways. The saddle turned, and the rider fell off. The horse proceeded to kick the saddle apart, and he was so upset that it took a week to catch him. He had also picked up a bad habit: when he felt a rider shift his weight in the saddle, he'd jump sideways and run away.

A big gelding spooked with me right where a hundred cows had bedded down. He slipped in the cow manure. I came off and kept hold of the reins to keep the horse's head pulled toward me so he wouldn't skid, swing his rear over, and step on me. This shot me down, and I landed flat on my back on a half-dozen huge, wet, cow piles.

A mare spooked and ran. The rider couldn't turn her. They had different ideas about which side of a tree to go around. The rider was slammed into the tree and nearly broke her back. She couldn't ride for a year.

A natural defense for the horse, zebra, deer, antelope, cow, goat, and such animals, is to spook and run away from anything real or imagined that might injure or kill them. These grass-eaters rely on speed, instinct, sight, and smell to give them the idea to leave *pronto.* The swift survive. It's been that way for millions of years, and we're not about to change it. We have to learn how to cope with it.

A flighty horse is much more prone to shy than his stolid take-everything-in-stride brethren. He lives in fear that something horrible might happen to him. In mares, the timid ones may fear a stallion, so they'll be a problem and, like the silent-heat mares, hard to settle. They need the more gentle stallions, and I think it's a good thing to stall such a mare near a stallion so that she gets to know him.

So it is with the trainer. the mare must learn to trust her trainer, or her life will be hell. A compassionate female trainer will usually handle such training duties better than a macho male. The timid horse, whether mare or gelding, won't bluff a rider and will seldom buck, but he may spook or run.

The fear a timid horse feels is very real. I've often turned the timid one back toward the spooky object and actually felt the heart pounding away under my leg. Whipping such a horse for shying is a great mistake, for you cause the horse to fear the rider as well as the object he shies from.

Riding the timid horse in the company of solid older horses is a prime method for training the fearful one. The terror-stricken horse observes his friends going along, fearing nothing, and learns from them. A person who can't recognize the fearful horse has no business training horses.

I like to reward horses with treats, and doing so is especially helpful with this type of animal. It reassures the timid horse, so that there's no mistaking the trainer's approval. If the timid one is too frightened to eat something he really likes, better back off and slow down.

"Conformation is everything." I quote my old guru, Charley Arujo. You have to have a good head and a good eye to have good conformation. Yet I've seen top judges pin horses that had poor eyes.

A statement I really believe is that the eye mirrors the soul, or, if you prefer, the disposition of the horse. A horse should have a large, calm, brown-rimmed eye, excepting albinos, Appaloosas, and so on. My horse Tengo Tivio has, in my opinion, a perfect eye, and his nature is calm. He has

Ranald Cameron on Tengo Tivio. Tengo was twenty-two years old when this was taken.

never hurt anyone or anything. A toddler, just walking, once crawled into Tengo's pen. The child tottered to the horse, grabbed him around a front leg, spun around, fell, and crawled under him. No problem. Tengo likes company.

The book *The Mind of a Horse* explains that a small-eyed horse gets a fuzzy picture and will spook at various objects. He's hard to handle in the wind, for he sees objects moving but can't tell what they are.

We had such a gelding to train at Meridian Meadows.

The owner was still there when the veterinarian we were using passed by the stall where the small-eyed horse was. "Where'd you get that pig-eyed bastard?" asked the friendly vet. I was flat mortified, for the owner was standing right there. Let me digress a bit. That episode amused all the riders, and from then on the colt was known as Ol' Pig Eye. I should have nipped that in the bud, but I didn't. Naturally they *had* to call the colt Ol' Pig Eye in front of the owner when he came for a visit. Double mortification! This has happened to me a lot, for we all have the bad habit of using descriptive nicknames.

We had a terrific palomino colt named Tivio's Stormy Blond. When he was a baby, his eyelids had a reddish tinge, and Dave Baggett started calling him "Otis." That colt was called Otis for eight months while I kept correcting the riders. They'd say, "Otis," and I'd yell, "Dammit, call him Stormy!" The name Stormy is used now, especially in my presence.

So, you trainers and would-be trainers, don't fall into the trap. If you have Terwilliger's Delicious Perennial in to train, call him "Deli" or something like that. Don't tag him with "Pig eye," "Nerd," "Runt," or other such names. You'll eventually get caught.

The small-eyed horse probably accounts for the largest number of spooky, problem horses. OK, he's small-eyed. Is he small-eyed and timid, or small-eyed and bold? Is he a bully, or is he bullied? Train accordingly. The timid horse must have great trust in his rider, while the rider must take strong measures with the bold or bullying-type horse.

Chapo was raised with a fine colt, Criol. One day Criol got caught in our smooth, wire fence and injured a hock. While the veterinarian was examining Criol, Chapo came up to investigate. The vet slapped him *lightly* on the muzzle to get him out of the way.

No human had ever done such a thing before, and this slight reprimand terrorized Chapo. When a human would approach, he'd rear straight up and tear around his stall with front hooves flailing away at the ceiling. He seemed to fear any human who was standing upright. I'd cut some good grass with my knife, go into the stall, bend way over, and offer him the grass. In this manner I gradually got him back to normal.

He was tough to start. We had to use colt bit and draw reins to maintain control. He'd set his neck and fall when pulled to the right. Once we tied him down after he fell. This helped to keep him on his feet during future rides, and he started going pretty well. Eventually, we got him into the hackamore.

One day Kenny Serco and I took Criol and Chapo for a long trail ride. Kenny was on Chapo. As we rode through pasture and forest, we realized that we had a tricky ditch-water crossing to navigate on the way back to the barn.

Many of the Colombian Paso colts were flighty. They'd spook but would seldom refuse to go anywhere if urged a bit. When we got to the water we had to cross, Criol paddled right on through, but Chapo refused to follow. I rode back and forth through the water to show Chapo he had nothing to fear, but there was no way to get him to follow his buddy.

For some time we'd been using a regular California hackamore with a twenty-two-foot mecate on Chapo. Kenny tied the reins up so the heel of the noseband wouldn't pull off Chapo's chin. He handed me the lead-rope end of the mecate and at my suggestion removed his chaps to use as a gentle persuader.

I led Chapo to the water from Criol's back. When Chapo refused to go down into the cutbank and into the water, Kenny "warped" Chapo's rump with his chaps. Startled, Chapo jumped down the bank, through the water, and up the other side. All this was a little swift for Criol, but we got the mess sorted out without injuring human or equine.

Since it was getting late, we rode on back to the barn. The next day we repeated the process until Chapo would "half-way" willingly go through water.

Why did it work? Think about the process we used to get the timid colt to cross water. He was with his best horse friend, who *would* cross water. He was persuaded with something that didn't hurt at all. I can think of no better way to get such a horse to cross water.

When a rider has to use something to whip a horse with in such a situation, the whip should perhaps frighten but shouldn't hurt. The doubled latigo popper is ideal, but I've seldom seen it used by anyone but me. Why not? Because most folks can't use them.

One must be able to hit what one wants to with the popper. I can use one to swat flies. The novice may hit himself or miss the horse entirely. The answer to this is fairly simple. Make a popper and practice using it.

When I was a kid, you could buy a toy gun made of heavy cardboard and paper. It was arranged so that a kid could point it at the sky and then whip it down to the horizon. It would make a satisfying loud crack.

The popper works like that. The two pieces of broad light leather crack together when banged down on a bronc's rump or shoulder. The scat bat works on the same principle, but it's heavier, hurts more, and doesn't make as much noise.

All you need is an old latigo piece about forty inches long. Double the latigo, fasten it together near the fold, and run the handle—a piece of rawhide shoelace—through the doubled end. Tie the string together, hook it over your middle finger and practice. Sit on a barrel and whack the barrel. When you can finally hit what you want to, you're ready to use it (rather than a whip that hurts) on a colt. I'd suggest that you whack your own leg with it a few times to get an idea of what kind of punishment you'll be dealing out.

When you need to move a colt out, and you happen to be wearing heavy chaps, whack your leather-covered leg instead of the colt. He'll move.

Bill Coleman was once trying to force a colt across water near my barn. He'd been trying for fifteen minutes or so without any luck. I grabbed my "fish" (saddle slicker) and walked out there. Bill kept the colt pointed at the water, and I whacked the colt over the rump with the slicker. The colt jumped into the water pronto. We made the colt cross back and forth over the creek a dozen times.

This can be dangerous. I've had several real wrecks, but the most unusual near wreck was with Fay. Fay was one of the most worthless horses I've had to deal with. Each trotting step she took was as hard as a buck jump. She had a propensity to rear, and, when she did so, she'd go straight up and teeter, just a whisper from going over backwards.

One day when I felt I needed a lot of pain, I took Fay for a long trail ride. She kept me so busy that I didn't think too far ahead. We had to cross an inch of water where it washed over a road. Fay refused to cross. I got off, found a twelve-foot-long tree branch, and brought it up back of her hocks. She crossed the water. I made her cross and recross many times.

Riding on at a walk, I realized that time was rapidly passing. I could take the rough water crossing where we'd had trouble with Chapo, or go back the way I came—in the dark. I opted to keep on going.

When we came near the tough crossing, Fay refused. I knew that I had to keep her going or she'd really stick, so I hooked the ol' popper over my finger and started warping her rump. The popper was cracking away in rapid-fire mode. All this action made her think about getting her rump whacked, and she forgot to rear.

When we got to the water, Fay leaped off the trail, reared, and wrapped both her front legs around each side of a large tree. She kept her hind legs working, which moved her around the tree, but the only thing on the other side of the tree was space. We dropped down about six feet into water. Fay started lunging to get out, and I pointed her at the opposite bank. We came through without a scratch on either of us, but I don't see how.

Fay kept up her bitchy ways. One day she reared up and teetered a dozen times with me. Enough! I threw her and tied her down. We draped a blanked over her, got some coffee and cookies, and had a coffee break. We rode other colts around her for the rest of the afternoon. When we untied her, she reared no more.

Fay was the hardest-trotting horse I ever rode. My knees would be rubbed raw on a long ride if I didn't wrap them with Ace bandages. Her owner had four fused vertebrae and needed a smooth Paso or Tennessee Walking Horse.

One fine Arabian filly was hauled to me. I liked everything about her when I looked her over. As I was leading her to a stall, she spooked and nearly ran over me. When I started riding her, she spooked badly at nearly everything. If I rode her along a fence, she'd jump ten feet sideways at fence-post shadows on the ground. Once she flattened a rider when she spooked at a place where a boat *used* to be.

I asked a veterinarian who was an equine specialist to look her over. He checked her eyes with an ophthalmoscope and discovered that the nerves into the eyes were so ragged it was doubtful that she could see much. He suggested that poor nutrition could have caused this condition. Her owner

Throwing Fay. One hind foot was scotch-hobbled short. Then the other hind foot was scotch-hobbled. She sat down.

was having a tough time getting the bills paid, so this could be true.

What should you do if your horse spooks at an object? Take him back to it, but *never* allow him to turn completely away from the object that spooked him. Let's say you're riding in a field and your horse shies at a log. He whirls to the right. Use your left rein to pull him back to the object. Use your right leg to keep him from moving to the right. Never allow him to make a complete circle to get back to the

241

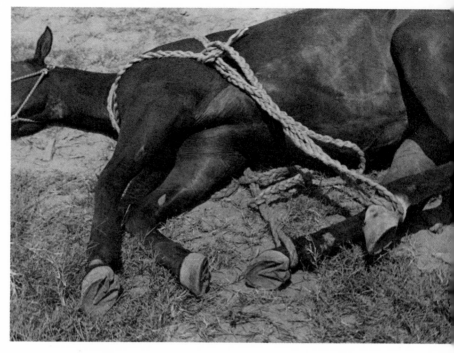

We pushed Fay over on her side. With both legs still secured, she couldn't kick, and we were pretty safe.

object, for it will teach him to turn away and run or to rear up when shying.

Wrong way: The horse shies at a log and whirls to the right. The rider makes him circle by using the right (direct) rein or the left (indirect, or neck) rein. The horse has turned completely away from the spooky object and thinks that it's now time to really run and put some distance between himself and the scary monster.

Right way: The horse spooks at the log and whirls to the right. The rider pulls the left rein and uses the right leg.

242

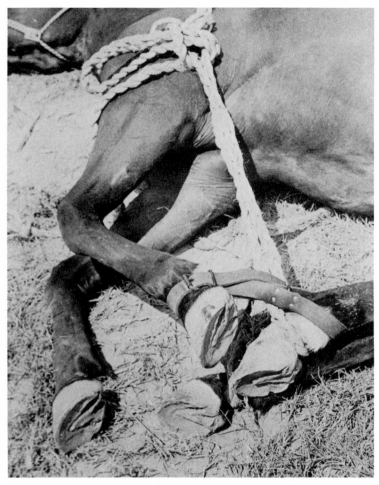

Straps, in this instance two Utah hobbles, secure Fay's left front leg to her left rear leg.

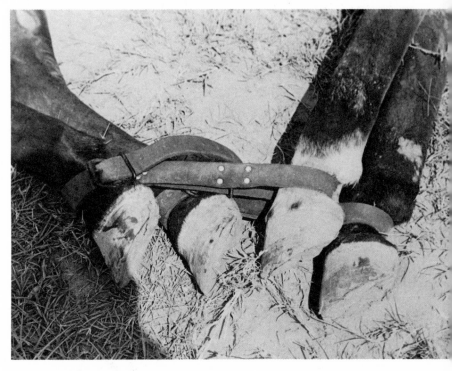

Both straps are in place. The scotch-hobble ropes are removed. The hobbles can be tied together to *make sure* the horse stays down. While she is in this position, her hooves can be raised for hoof trimming or shoeing. The easy way to do this is to lay a two-by-four over her back and under the hobbles and then lift the hooves. One man works the lumber, while the other trims or shoes.

The horse is pulled back to face the object. He has whirled only 40 degrees or less before being brought back. He can't run, for he'd have to run toward the object. He can be legged up to the object, shown that it won't hurt him, and so forth.

To correct the shying horse, a bit whereby you use the

Jimmy Lee Thomas sacks Fay out. She has no chance to get up. A blanket is under her head to make a soft pad and keep sand out of her eyes.

direct rein is essential. He will disobey the neck rein, and a curb-type bit should be used only with the indirect rein, the neck rein.

Let's say the horse shies at a log while wearing the curb bit. The rider pulls him back with the left (indirect) rein. The leverage of the curb bit pulls the bit down on the tongue and bars, causing intense pain. The horse rears and falls on the rider.

245

Now let's say the horse is wearing the colt bit or hacka-more (rawhide, not mechanical). He shies at a log and whirls. The rider again uses the left rein. There is no leverage and little pain. The horse is pulled back to face the spooky object. He stops, snorts, and is assured by the rider that the object won't hurt him. My barn is a training barn. We use few curb bits. They're for the finished, older horses or such self-workers as cutting or rope horses. When we use curb-type bits, they're Pelhams, and two reins are used. When a horse has to be pulled, the top rein is used, and there is no pain to make the colt go crazy.

I couldn't begin to write about all the times I've had to double a colt on this top rein to stop him from spooking and running away.

# 21. Tail Wringers and Head Tossers

A famous old-time bronc rider found a fine stallion during his travels. He bought the horse and had him hauled to the home ranch. He sent instructions to leave the horse alone until he got home.

When he had a little space between shows, he drove home and took a second look at the horse he'd purchased. He wasn't disappointed. That was one fine stallion.

The horse was supposed to be broke, so he saddled up and climbed aboard. The horse *was* broke, but he continually wrung his tail. This was disappointing, for no cowboy likes to ride a tail wringer.

The bronc man, his brother, a couple of hired hands, and a neighbor all discussed tail wringers and the best methods for correcting them. A plan was thought out and discarded. Another idea made no sense. Finally the neighbor came up with one that had possibilities. He thought the tail should be weighted down.

After scrounging around for something that would work, they eventually found a couple of horn weights and tied them on the stallion's tail. The owner mounted the horse to give it a try.

All of this went on inside a bronc pen with sides made of upright posts eight feet high. When the horse started to trot around the pen, he tried to wring his tail. The heavy horn weights flipped around and smashed the horse in the testicles. The stud dropped his head, let out a bawl, and bucked clear up on top of that eight-foot fence. The bronc man fell off and dropped outside the pen. He was dazed and just lay there.

The bronc teetered on top of the fence and finally fell outside, where he landed all over the bronc rider, breaking quite a few of the rider's bones and smashing him up in general. When the bronc man finally was able to navigate again, he told his friends that he'd be a little more choosey about where he got his advice in the future.

Most tail wringing doesn't produce such dramatic results, but it is annoying and shows that the horse is agitated. Lyle Christie, Charley Araujo's early partner, once said in a letter that he'd been to a big horse show where "the air was made cool on an otherwise unbearably hot day by the wringing of a thousand tails." I doubt it was that bad.

A man brings a colt to me for training. He hasn't done much with him, but he wants the colt to look like a fine show horse. He pulls the tail, trims the nose whiskers, trims out the ears, and cuts a bridle track.

The colt, who is used to a certain weight and length to his tail, now finds it too short to hit all the flies he aims at, so he has to experiment to learn how to sight in on them again.

In the spring we start getting heat, humidity, and bugs in Florida. Little kids run around all squinty-eyed as they try to play and keep gnats out of their eyes. Yet the colt owner had trimmed out his colt's ears so that all manner of bugs could get in them. The bugs get caught in ear wax, buzz, and stomp around, and the colt slings his head and wrings his tail in annoyance.

With the bridle track all neatly trimmed, the hackamore headstalls slip all over the place, so browbands have to be rigged immediately. All this just to look neat.

We start handling the colt. The saddle doesn't fit. No

saddle fits a colt perfectly, for their backs are all different. You'd have to take a mold of his back and make saddle bars to fit it. This just isn't done. There are pressure points that irritate him. If he's round-backed and low-withered, he'll have to put up with a tight cinch. Put all this together and you see why some colts wring their tails.

A client brought me a filly who had had all this stuff done to her. On top of that her rump was a foot higher than her withers, so the saddle kept sliding onto her neck. She was long-backed, and it looked as though the rider was actually sitting on her withers. She was grouchy to boot and somewhat ewe-necked, so her head was high. With her teeth bared in a snarl, her front hooves stamping displeasure, her tail wringing like a fan, and the rider trying to stay upright while sitting on her withers, it was a helluva sight.

We had a lot of things to do in a hurry, or we'd spoil that filly pronto. I ordered a long-seated Rawlide tree and had it a couple of days later. We set it on her and noted that it rested on her shoulder blades. I put a rotary rasp in a drill and cut the material away at those high spots.

I also noted that full double rigging wasn't going to do it. By making forward-cut skirts, I managed to rig in the skirts and get the rigging three or four inches forward of full double. I gave this project top priority, and in less than a week I had the saddle ready.

In the meantime, the riders were thinning some long tails. We started tying a fake tail on the filly, and before long she had a long, full tail again.

I built a high front on that saddle, but in use there was still a little downward slope toward her withers. Still, we could ride her, which wasn't possible before we had the new saddle.

I made her a double-rope bosal, one rope above the other.

This made a wide, flat noseband. We set it very low, so that it allowed her rider to hackamore her and keep her nose low. We didn't want to bother her with a bit.

She had to be kept as happy as possible. The bosal noseband was long so she could chew a treat while being ridden. We'd slice carrots down the middle and cut them into chunks so she wouldn't choke on them.

The filly's attitude changed. She started enjoying work, for she loved carrots, and she was more comfortable in the new saddle. It was hard to wring that long, full, heavy, tail, and it was more fun to be nice. We trained her pretty well in the six months we had her here.

Why go to all this trouble? Why not just send her home as impossible to train and get on with better ones? Well, it's a challenge. I don't like to send one home if there's any possible way to get him working. I'll send a horse home if I think he's insane and might seriously hurt someone, either here or later down the road. When I get a bad one who's wider between the nostrils than the eyes, I consider sending him home. If he'll kill himself in order to kill a rider, I don't want anything to do with him.

Over the years, I've had many trainers call me about these insane horses as a sort of last resort. They hate to admit they're stumped.

Without exception they are bad-headed horses with very little room for normal-sized brains. They have no regard for their own skins and will commit suicide when fighting a rider.

Once I was riding a loco bronc (made so by eating locoweed). I'd ridden him a little too hard, and he got sweaty. He started bucking and leaped right out into space near the top of a mountain. Boy, what a wreck. I was very lucky to walk away from that one.

This horse was crazy because he was weedy; others are

crazy because they're so poorly bred. Don't waste your time or your neck fooling with them.

High-headed horses and head slingers are two different things, but in one respect they could receive the same treatment. Whether ridden English or western, they can have their heads held down by artificial (gimmicky) means. In English practice a standing martingale is used. Westerners use a tie-down.

If an English hunter or jumper needs a standing martingale, his rider thinks nothing of using such gear. The western barrel racer, roper, or steer wrestler uses a tie-down as a matter of course. A calf roper says his horse can lean into the noseband and stop better if a tie-down is used. If this is the case, then use a flat leather or padded tie-down. Don't use a wire or thin cable tie-down. If you want to train a high-headed horse or a head tosser and then discard the tie-down, the severe one might be used *once.*

My brother Dan swapped around and ended up with a little mare who couldn't even navigate without a tie-down. She'd wreck your face when you got on or off. She'd flip and flop around, stumbling and falling, without that tie-down. The mare was very likable, so I decided to wire her head down. I made a wire tie-down, set it midway up her nose, mounted, and reined her around for a few minutes. When I took it off, she didn't need a tie-down. She also had a very sore nose for a week. That happened in 1955, and I haven't wired one since.

Some horses are high-headed because of poor conformation. A ewe-necked horse's neck is hollow at the top and rigid at the bottom. It's difficult for him to flex his neck, so the head goes up. Solution: Use a padded tie-down if the horse's head position is confirmed. Use a running martingale to try to correct the condition. Some form of bit that has a cricket might help.

Bill Levitz on an Arabian stallion. He is using double reins, Pelham bit, and running martingale.

Arabians, Saddlebreds, Tennessee Walkers, some Morgans, Thoroughbreds, and others have naturally high head carriage because of the laid-back slope of their shoulders. The tall Thoroughbred Quarter Horse has this tendency. Trainers of western pleasure horses sometimes set their horses' heads in a hangdog position that I think looks ridiculous. The horse's head carriage is determined by his conformation. When you go against nature, you offend your Maker. Going against

Bill Levitz on a dun gelding. He is using a colt bit, bit guard, and draw reins.

nature is faddish. Before long people will revolt against you (or should).

Some years ago we had a nice Arabian gelding who had been semispoiled with rush presale training. At a canter the horse would throw up his head and go where he pleased. The condition was firmly implanted. We used a running martingale that kept the reins low on this horse. He couldn't resist the pull of the low rein and worked fair from the start. As

253

we used it more, he lightened up and worked very well. After a year we no longer needed the running martingale.

There are two different ways to rig draw reins to correct both head tossers and high-headedness. The regular draw reins are tied or snapped to the cinch rings and run up through the bit rings and back to the rider. The pull is low, and the double action of the reins increases the rider's power. Most horses can be turned around when this kind of draw rein is used. *Always* use some form of bit guard when using this draw rein. You can hurt a horse by pulling the bit into or clear through his mouth if you don't use a guard. If you hurt him enough, he may hurt you. *Never use a draw rein on a curb bit.*

There's much less need for the polo draw rein, because a running martingale does the same job with less chance of injury. There are cases, however, when it works very well, for the action of any draw rein is smooth, since the rein runs over the bit ring rather than being attached to it.

To rig it, you need a strap that hooks to the center bar of your cinch or loops over the center of the cinch. There's a ring at the other end of this strap. It should rest at the center of the chest. Another strap around the neck holds the ring in place. Two reins fasten to the ring, run through the bit rings, and go on back to the rider.

Let's try this rig on a high-headed horse. Set the polo draw so the horse can *escape pressure by flexing correctly.* Let him alone until he stops fighting and starts flexing. This might take two hours or two months. When he'll stand in his stall and flex rather than fight, take him to the riding pen and rig him the same way. Leave him alone to see if he'll flex. OK? Now lead him to see if he'll flex. OK? Now longe him at a walk and trot. He'll try to pop his nose. Don't rush. When he accepts all this, ride him. In time he'll improve as far as his mind and conformation will let him.

Salinas bit with small bosal that goes under the bridle.

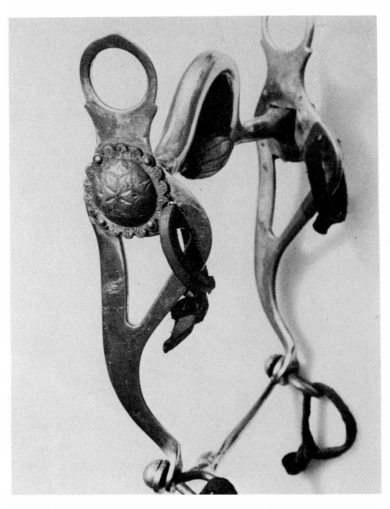

Plain Salinas bit. Note that holes have been drilled in the bit so that double reins can be used.

A good California bit with Salinas or Mona Lisa mouth might be helpful eventually, for most horses love to work the crickets in these bits. When working such bits, the horse will slobber. This is desirable because it helps the horse keep a good mouth. In Colombia a horse that doesn't make mouth moisture is eliminated from a class. In Chapter 5 of this book I mention revamping a spade bit for such work.

# 22. Falling Horses

THE horse who falls on his rider is one of the most dangerous animals a person can handle. There's little chance of the rider's escaping injury or death. It can happen as the result of a forward somersault, a high rear in which the horse just keeps coming over, or as a deliberate act whereby the horse throws itself sideways to land squarely on the rider. I've never had the latter happen to me.

Glen Lillibridge, a former apprentice of mine, was a long time getting off crutches. He had his ankle shattered when a horse flipped over on him. He leaped to get away, but one foot hung in a stirrup.

David Bagett, a recent apprentice, was lying in the arena when I returned from town one day. The ambulance was there and the attendants were trying to make some sense out of what he was mumbling: "Well, now what happened? What horse was it? There's nothin' here that could throw me, is there? Did a horse fall on me?"

They took him to the hospital. He wouldn't stay in bed or wear a hospital gown, so they sent him home after three days. He still couldn't keep food down (he had been fed intravenously at the hospital).

In a few days he was trying to walk but was dragging a leg. I sent him to a veterinarian who had a laser. After a couple of treatments, he had feeling and warmth in his leg again. Since the treatments involved an area in the lower back, I reckoned that the cantle hit him there. In all probability the filly he'd been working had lost footing with her

A horse ready to somersault on a rider.

front hooves and had turned a forward flip on him. This happens in a split second. A rider has no chance to get away.

It happened to me about 1970. My rider, Ken Serco, had gone out to fetch a mare and colt. The mare had foaled a month early, and the other mares were trying to steal her colt. I had to go somewhere with the boss. When we got back, Ken was still out in the pasture somewhere. I got a little panicky and grabbed a filly out of the first stall. Slapping a saddle and hackamore on her, I started loping across a long pen toward the pasture gate.

259

Then the ground shot up at me, and I felt a lot of pain. The filly had flipped forward, and I was under her. She struggled to her feet. I was lying on my back across the saddle with one foot in the stirrup. After a couple of staggering lurches, she fell all over me again. I felt horn and cantle wham against my back, the saddle horn against my spine. When she did get up, I was free of her, but I was lying there ground into the sand. I felt like Beetle Bailey after Sarge works him over.

Cautiously I started moving my fingers. They worked. Then I tried moving my arms and legs. They moved. Finally I tried lifting and turning my head. All parts seemed to be functioning.

I made it to my hands and knees. The world was spinning a little but soon slowed down and stopped. Lurching to my feet, I tried to walk but fell down. As I tried again, I saw Kenny coming with the mare and colt. He'd had a few problems but nothing important.

To this day my back pops out of place if I bend over. To put it right, I'll lie down on some hay bales and put rolled-up feed sacks under each shoulder. All one needs to do to adjust my upper back is to use about six ounces of force. It'll click, pop, and go back in place.

Such wrecks over the years have taken their toll. I consider myself lucky, however. If I'd had a saddle with the little dinky sharp horn that modern barrel racers and cutting-horse riders use, I'd be dead or crippled. That small horn's lethal in bad situations.

A wreck like this can happen whenever you work a horse at speed. You can be cutting cattle when your colt will get cut down by a calf that turns into his front legs. You can be roping when a calf will fall in front of your horse. Or a clumsy colt will simply stub a toe and fall all over you. You can't prepare for it, and you can't get away from the horse, for it happens in a split second.

You can be as careful as possible. Roll (bevel) the toes on the colts you work. Try to train your horses to be natural-headed, not stargazers. If you use a tie-down or other equipment to keep a stargazer's head down, make sure that equipment is in first-class order. Sell those clumsy horses. If you have to train a clumsy one, pay attention to what you're doing every second you're on him.

Art Williams was an old cowboy I rode with in Colorado. I had a horse in my string who had to be ridden with a tie-down. Without it he'd stampede and probably fall.

Once while Art was riding this particular horse, he was chasing a cow down a mountain. The tie-down broke, and the horse fell. What saved Art was that he was able to flap his arms and "fly" away from the horse while they were sailing through the air. They flew fifty feet before touchdown and then rolled down the mountain to the bottom. Art had to borrow a company saddle after that wreck, for there was nothing left of his.

I thought my tie-down was in pretty good shape, but this horse threw his head up with tremendous force, and the tie-down broke. At the time I was trying to get around a cow to turn her. We were racing through dense aspen trees. When the tie-down broke, the horse shot forward. His head went so high that the bits were upside down, and they weren't designed to work in that position. He shot between two trees, which he barely cleared. Unfortunately I didn't.

My heavy chaps saved me from breaking my knees in those trees. When I hit the trees, I was forced from the saddle. I managed to grab the horn and held onto it. I was laid straight out on that horse's back doing the Cossack death drag like the very best trick riders do. The horse, not being trained for trick riding, kicked up. This popped me way up in the air, and I dropped down into the saddle as neatly as you'd want to see. I managed to pull one rein and got the horse circling. When he hit a big aspen head first, he stopped in one motion. Sad to say, there was no one around to witness these great equestrian feats except some old rank cows that didn't seem to give a hoot. I cut off all my saddle strings and tied them together to patch up the tie-down.

There is usually some reason why a horse rears up and falls backwards. Ordinarily the rider who decides to leave the horse to his own devices has a chance to get off, for this rearing up and falling over is slower than a forward flip at speed.

Needless to say, a person who trains his horse to rear up is playing with death. Those movie horses may look fancy when they rear, but they know what they're doing, and even some trained horses get carried away, slip, and fall over backwards.

Some horses are, or become, cinchy. They're often called "cinch binders." They're so "cold-backed" that they may go up and over when you first mount up. *Cinch* is the clue. Never use a cheap or dirty cinch. Make sure the center bar isn't all humped up from dirt and horse sweat so that it causes pain.

When you cinch up, you'll often see some bunched or wrinkled skin under the cinch. This bothers some horses. To straighten out the skin, lift the horse's front legs and pull them straight forward.

Make sure your cinch is long enough for the cinch rings to clear the horse's elbows. Make sure your cinch isn't too wide, or it will rub the elbows. You shouldn't use more than a nineteen-strand cinch with a full double-rigged saddle.

I use cinch chafes (guards). The latigo makes a lump over the cinch rings. The more wraps you take with your latigo, the bigger the lump will be. I use only clean mohair cinches. We make our own, and we sew the center bar on the outside so that it won't have a big lump to it that might irritate a horse. We also make the cinch chafes, and they go on every cinch we use.

We use good, flat-plate cinch buckles. When the cinch gets old and starts to fray, we cut the cords off the buckles and re-cord it, making a new cinch.

When you're used to latigos made of latigo leather, don't switch and use nylon. The nylon slips, and because it tightens easier, you may tighten too much.

If you get a new horse, take some time cinching him up until you know him well. Cinch up just tight enough so the saddle won't slip. Walk him around a little, every once in a while tightening the cinch a little bit more until you get it where you want it. When you put your toe in the stirrup, watch the horse. If he backs up, don't get on. Just hop along with him until he stops. *Never* get up on a horse when he's backing.

Check your saddle. If it's too narrow or doesn't fit your horse, it will pinch him. He might buck, or he might rear up. How do you check it? Look at the way it rests on his back. Does it snug right down or sit up high? Use an acrylic poly pad. These really sweat a horse's back. After he's been worked, you may see dry spots. They're where he's being pinched.

We've had this problem recently. The acrylic pad showed us that the horse was being pinched along the back of his left shoulder blade. Going to a wider saddle solved the problem.

A horse may learn to rear in response to irritation from a sore, but will keep it up even after a properly fitting saddle is used. He's learned to rear when, say, loping circles. He's used to getting pinched then, and will rear even though there's no pain. When this happens, I have a rider work the horse in the breaking pen. I stand in the center with a longe whip. If the horse stops and tries to rear, I drive him forward by tapping him with the whip. Before long his rider can carry a crop and just tap the horse if he acts as though he'll stop and rear.

One of the most mysterious things a horse does is suddenly slam on the brakes and rear up for no apparent reason. Any number of things can cause this sort of behavior. A large bug can fly into his eye, hitting the eyeball with great force. This is a common occurrence in Florida. Or a bug can go into the ear (I don't like to have owners trim out the ears before bringing a colt to me; a bushy ear goes a long way toward keeping bugs out). Even more common is the colt's habit of playing with the bit. He'll get his tongue over the mouthpiece, and the bit will clunk down on sensitive bars of his mouth. The sudden pain shocks him, so he slams on the brakes and rears.

This sudden action can really startle the rider, who may automatically jerk the reins, hurting the colt a great deal more and possibly causing him to rear up and fall over. To prevent this, tie the bit up in the mouth, or try one of my bit guards that can be set to hold the colt bit high against the roof of the mouth. The bit is gradually lowered as the colt learns about it. At English tack stores you can buy a rubber "spade" to slip on a snaffle bit. Or you can run a thong through the bit rings and mouthpiece of a snaffle. This can be tied to the forelock or the top of the headstall (à la Ed Connell).

Canine and wolf teeth are a problem. If a bit hits one of these teeth with force, the horse may stop and rear. A veterinarian can extract wolf teeth and saw off canine teeth. It's usually the upper canine teeth that cause the problem. This is a male-horse problem, and these teeth need to be cut off or removed when the horse is five or six years old.

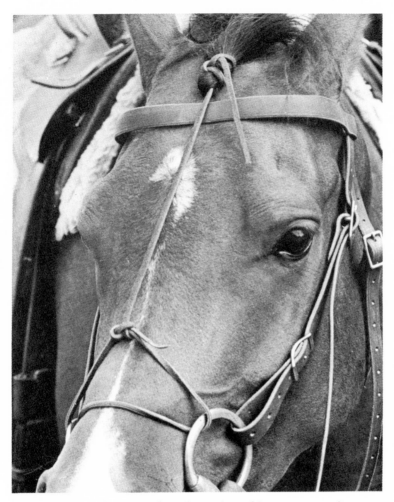
How to tie a snaffle bit so the colt won't get his tongue over it.

Overbitting a horse can cause problems. Let's say the colt is used to a hackamore or colt bit. A rider may suddenly bit him with a curb and try to stop him hard. He'll hurt the colt, perhaps pulling him over backwards.

When a new leverage hackamore device came out, a California cowboy who wasn't any Einstein bought one and tried it on his horse. He ran him out and set back on the new hackamore. When he woke up, he was in the hospital, for the colt had stopped all right—and rolled on over backwards.

If one sets back on one rein of a curb-bit bridle, he'll cause a horse much pain. The horse will probably go up in the air and may fall on over. That is why I'm high on Pelhams and don't care much for straight curb bits.

When a horse runs or does something else as bad, the rider should be able to double the horse right around in his tracks. If the rider simply hauls back on a curb bit, he'll just cause pain, which, of course, makes a horse rear.

# 23. Some Really Tough Problems

## HORSES WHO BULLY TIMID PEOPLE

WE'RE always getting questions from people whose horses just won't respect them, move out for them, or cooperate with them. There's no ready answer to this. The small, novice rider should have a willing older horse with good, confirmed habits. Many children and novice grown-ups are bullied by young horses, who sense the owner's lack of bravery and strength.

I've often written about Dixie and Becky. Becky "just had to have" Dixie, a two-year-old Quarter filly with a slight bit of training. The filly was boarded with us. Becky was bucked down hard a dozen times before she told me about her problem. I suggested putting the filly in training for a few months, and Becky's parents agreed.

Dixie was no problem at all. She cooperated 100 percent. We used her to check pastures, roped off of her, anything. One day I showed Becky how well the filly handled. She wanted to try her. It was the same old thing. Dixie would poke around at a snail's pace or buck.

This brought on the tears. Becky loved Dixie and didn't understand that Dixie didn't give a hoot about her love and wouldn't work for her. We had a long talk about it. The horse's brain—how a horse thinks—isn't like a human brain.

We would never have considered Dixie a bully, however, if we hadn't known about how she reacted to Becky. Dixie did anything you asked of her and did it willingly. Did she sense that I wouldn't tolerate her silliness, or was it a case of bad vibrations with Becky? *Quien sabe?* We never abused Dixie, never roughed her up.

Our solution was to talk Becky into selling Dixie. I found a willing, gentle mare for her, and the love affair with a horse had a better chance. Another solution could have been to lend Dixie to a rider for a few years until good habits became second nature, and Dixie became a solid, willing mare. Naturally, Becky's parents couldn't afford to keep the mare in training until Dixie matured.

Humans tend to idealize horses as well as to humanize them. If we humanize them, we should admit that horses are good and bad, for people are good and bad. The best people in the world certainly harbor rotten thoughts once in a while. To be good, the good person rises above such thoughts. Should the horse be able to do the same? Not always. The gentle horse *can* blow up. The person who has lived a long life with horses has seen this happen many times.

There are bad horses, horses who would be regular man-eaters if they weren't afraid of retribution. They'd like to hurt or wipe out people, but they don't want to get hurt in return. Such horses will bully anyone if they can get away with it.

My first real horsebreaking job came about during the tail end of World War II. Some big shots bought a load of horses condemned by the cavalry. They hired me to straighten them out so they could end up with a few good saddle horses and sell off the surplus.

I bought one of those horses myself. The dealer gypped me; he lied about the purchase price and about the horse. The horse was an old outlaw who had been not only an artillery horse but also a saddle bronc in quite a few rodeos before I was suckered into buying him.

The barn where I was going to keep this bronc was about

four miles down a highway from where he was stabled. I decided to ride him home. When I got on him, he started bucking and running. I didn't know what to do about such a thing, so I pointed him toward the home barn. We traveled those four miles that way. I had a very interested parade of autos following me the whole way.

Frankly, I don't know how I managed to ride that horse so far. I was so sore and scared of him that I didn't go to the barn for a week. The farmer who owned the place told me the stall had been kicked apart three times that week. I had to tame that horse pronto or find some other place to keep him.

Back then we had no bronc pens to ride in. I saddled the horse and rode him into a back pasture. He seemed all right at a walk and trot. When I tried to lope him, he blew the plug.

That ol' horse was a kicking bucker. He'd leave the ground and kick straight up behind. The first hard jump landed me on the saddle horn. I saw fire, lightning, and felt a helluva lot of pain. I came down in the saddle and came down fighting mad.

Both spurs connected with that bronc's shoulders, and I dragged them way back. I was yipping away with my war whoop, and horse hair was flying in the breeze. That bronc's head shot up, and the bucking stopped right then. He thought he had an easy one, but the tables were turned. From that point on, he behaved like a good one. Whenever I rode him, I showed him that my first name was Tiger. But I didn't want a horse I had to manhandle that way, and soon I sold him.


BALKING AND SULKING

There are many reasons why a horse will balk or sulk: inadequate preparation, ill-fitting gear, overriding (getting a young one too tired), or plain old horse rebellion against working for the human. No matter the cause, the problem is dangerous.

Many years ago I was breaking colts for a dude ranch near Cripple Creek, Colorado. The owner was getting senile and causing problems. His word was law, and things had to be done his way.

On a long horse drive from Woodland Park to Cripple Creek, one rider was given a bronc to use. We were just starting out on that ranch and weren't told that the filly had never been ridden before. After ten miles her belly was so raw from the cinch that she sulked. I roped another horse for the rider, and he changed mounts on the spot. Chalk up one spoiled horse. She was laid up all season. We broke her in the fall, and she turned out to be a pretty fair working horse, though she didn't trust humans and bucked every ride.

After I got a few colts started, the boss looked them over and picked a nice two-year-old filly for himself. A few days later he caught the filly, saddled up, and took a bunch of guests ten miles cross country to Pike's Peak, went up the mountain, and then rode back to the ranch. He wore the filly out. The only reason she didn't sulk with him was that she wanted to stay with the other horses. When he caught her next time, she sulked, and I got her back. Sulk and buck! She never turned out to be much. Chalk up *two* spoiled ones.

The ranch was sold that fall. It's a good thing. The boss turned those two fillies into sulkers and fighters because he didn't have any feeling for them. I never punished them for balking, and they eventually (more or less) got over it. They were *made* into sulkers. Some horses come by it naturally. They're born that way. Stern discipline is called for when handling such animals. Give them the benefit of the doubt first. Then get after them. If they don't get straightened out, they'll hurt or kill someone.

Sometimes broncs are so weird they're frightening. They

seem to be listening to voices from afar. A wiry old man once brought such a filly to me. The local horseshoer told me that this ol' boy broke his own horses but that this particular filly had thrown the old man clear over a fence.

Right from the first I knew I had a halfhearted sulker. She'd go so far and then refuse to move. Part of this came from ignorance. She didn't know what I wanted her to do. I broke her to drive, and that seemed to help.

Every ride, she'd hit one very hard buck jump. There would be no warning, and it'd really shake me up. It seemed to knock her so silly she couldn't keep it up. I couldn't get her to stop it.

One cold day I saddled her and turned her loose in the bronc pen to run around and limber up while I cleaned her stall. When I returned to ride her, I noticed that she hadn't moved at all and was looking rather starry-eyed. When I walked up to her, she exploded and bucked straight into a post. The heavy hackamore noseband hit first. She flopped over backwards and looked dead as a horse could look.

Finally she wiggled a little, raised her head, laid it back down, and then surged up to stand looking at me in a very attentive fashion. When I examined her, I saw that she'd hit the post with such force that it knocked the hide off right down to the bone. I put healing salve on her injury, raised the hackamore up off the injured area, got on, and rode off. She never bucked or sulked again. In fact, she seemed very eager to please me.

When the ol' boy came to pick her up, I asked him to ride her. Of course, I rode her first and showed him she was working well. He finally got on her, and I could tell he was full of fear. He was so surprised to find that she'd work well for him that he made only a halfhearted attempt to beat me out of my training fee.

When this filly blew up in the pen, she received a blow on

the nose that almost killed her. She must have associated me with that huge knock on the head, though I wasn't even near her at the time. In any event, she was really cured.

A wealthy horse owner brought a spoiled one to me at the same place. He said there was nothing wrong with his filly, but I doubted that since he had his own trainer and wasn't likely to spend money on another one for the fun of it. He had a reputation for being very close with his dollars. When I tried the filly, she worked for a half hour and then sulked. Couldn't move her at all. Next day she shortened her working period. Before long she balked after five minutes of work.

I called the owner and told him what I thought the problem was. I said I could possibly cure it but that I wasn't going to anything to the filly unless he was present. Before long he showed up.

I saddled the filly and worked her a few minutes before she sulked. He said she wasn't any good like that and gave me the OK to attempt a cure. So I rigged her to drive as she stood there.

When I was ready, I slapped her on her fanny with a long line. Like most true balkers, she threw herself over backwards. I held her down by keeping one rein tight, which kept her head up in the air. I had him hold the rein while I tied her down. I put padding under her head so she wouldn't bang an eye if she fought. She did fight the foot ropes a few times. I rolled her over so both sides were worked. When she ceased struggling, I let her up and rode off on her. She never again balked. This guy tried to beat me out of a month's training fee on the grounds that he had helped me.

The cure for a balker is fairly obvious. Though he's balking, he *can* move if he has to. Take that away from him and he's got to give up. You don't need to pull him over when he rears or anything like that. There's no call for all that rough stuff. Your veterinarian can cast him and tie him

down for you. Don't abuse the horse when he's down, although sacking him out doesn't hurt anything. *Do* make sure that he doesn't get hot. If you are doing this during hot weather, cool off the bronc with a hose. Don't tie him down right after or just before food, for he could become upset and develop colic. And don't do it when you're angry.


WHEN IT'S NECESSARY TO THROW A HORSE

A fellow once wrote to a horse magazine that featured my stuff and said, "Dave Jones only knows one way to train horses and that's to throw and tie them down." Maybe I sound that way sometimes, but it's the spectacular that we remember. Reforming bad horses is something that has to be done, or they'll end up in cans.

A few folks have called or written to me about their inability to throw their horses. I've suggested that they have their vets do it. These people replied that their vets wouldn't cast a horse without giving him an anesthetic to knock him down. Obviously the horse shouldn't be thrown in such a fashion, for he must remember what's done to him.

One night a lady called and thanked me profusely for describing why and how to throw a horse. She owns a stallion who is dangerous. After the horse had been thrown and tied down, he changed dramatically. He now seems very safe to handle.

Here are some techniques for throwing a horse:

1. I was reminded of this old-time method after reading a book by an Australian who had handled broncs all of his long life. I had seen this done in Nebraska long ago but had forgotten about it. You blindfold the bronc and slap him on the neck. This startles him, and he begins to spin.

He falls, and there he will lie as long as the blindfold is in place. This works once per horse. After it's been done once, most broncs will refuse to spin. The danger in throwing a horse like this is that he may fall into something and injure himself, for he spins wildly all over the place. A sand-filled, solid-board breaking pen is an ideal place to throw a horse by this method.

2. A front leg may be strapped up and the horse turned the other direction. I don't care much for this method, because many things can go wrong while the bronc has only a single foreleg restrained.

3. For regular casting apparatus you need two long ropes and two foot straps. Make rope collars. Run the ropes through the rings on the foot straps, which are buckled on the back pasterns. Then run the ropes back up through the collars. When a strong man, or strong men, pulls on the ropes, the bronc's hind legs will be drawn forward and he'll go down. This is a version of a vet's casting rig.

4. Front hobbles and two ropes make a good rig. The ropes are run from the hobbles through the rings on the back foot straps and back around the hobbles. When the ropes are pulled, the four hooves are drawn together.

5. Scotch-hobble one hind leg and draw it up. Then scotch-hobble the other hind leg. When you pull on the second rope, the bronc will sit down like a dog. Quickly tie the second scotch-hobble rope. Push the bronc over onto his side. This is a pretty good method, for the bronc can't take a hard swipe at you with a hind hoof. It's a little tough tying him down correctly when the scotch-hobble ropes are still on his legs. Gripping the flank skin hard, with both hands, temporarily makes it impossible for him to kick. This works like a rope around the flank, paralyzing the rear end when drawn tight (anything really tight around the flank immobilizes the rear end). This flank grip makes it possible

not only to tie the bronc securely but also to remove the ropes safely when the session is over.

6. Sometimes we get an unhandled, rank colt who strikes or kicks any time the trainer gets close. You might catch the colt around the neck and use the lariat as the Australian Jeffery control rope, or you can forefoot him and then throw and tie him down—if you're roper enough to do so. Rather than risk having my head removed from my body by a real torpedo, I'd forefoot him.

Once I forefooted a stud in such a slick fashion that I can't believe I did it. A rank paint stud, he decided he'd had enough of me and lunged for my throat when I opened his stall to feed him. My guardian angel was with me that time. Something said, "Jump!" and I threw myself backwards as I saw this form leaping toward me. As it was, he got a little skin at my throat, but I've cut myself worse than that shaving.

I did a neat backward somersault out of his stall. A lariat was hanging on a pen in the aisle, and I grabbed for it as I came to my feet. I made a loop as I ran toward the breaking pen, which was attached to one end of the barn. That dang horse was chasing me.

Jumping aside just outside the barn, I spotted a loop at his front legs as he jumped into the pen. I caught them, flipped he rope, and took a hip lock on it. Ol' Paint went down, and I tied him to lie with the lariat. Colts were ridden around him all afternoon while he ate humble pie. When I finally untied him, he was reformed and never again made a bad move against me.

A lot of trainers today just take a club and tear up the horses they're unhappy with. I never had to beat a horse, because I knew other ways. I've never thrown or tied down a horse when I was *really angry,* and I don't believe a horse's disposition was ever ruined because I got after him.

275

Another rank stud, a huge Andalusian, had no respect for humans and liked to ridicule them. He was a tough one, and the only way I knew to fracture his ego was to throw him and tie him down. He tried to get me, but a lariat and a snubbing post stopped him. A helper and I threw and tied him down. When I let him up, he was a different horse. He had gained respect for people.

Training him wasn't difficult. Once in a while I'd go out in his paddock with him. He'd come to meet me. When I scratched his withers, he'd put his head on my shoulder and sigh with delight. If I'd kept him around very long, I'd probably have made a pet out of him.

# 24. Selection and Care of the Saddle

THE girl was very serious as she eased her toe into the stirrup and swung up onto the colt. The bay gelding shook his head, snorted, and gingerly walked away. He walked around the barnyard for ten minutes before the girl asked him to trot. He trotted a few steps, kicked sideways, and trotted on. Finally she asked him to canter. The bay colt bogged his head, bucked hard, and threw the girl. As she staggered to her feet, tears seeped from her eyes. This wasn't the first time the colt had bucked her off. She loved him but she was learning to fear him.

I've seen this problem many times. A child begs for a horse, and the parents finally agree. Not wanting to buy an old saddle, but still wanting to save money, they buy a new "cheapie." It doesn't fit the colt. When he tries to canter, the saddle digs into him, and he responds by shedding his rider.

One such rider had always wanted a horse and finally managed to move to an area where this was possible. She was given a cheap saddle and, not having worlds of money, decided to train him herself. Thank God, the colt was naturally gentle. Even so, he was soon bucking and rearing in response to the pain. He slipped the saddle once, and it was impossible to saddle him the next time. The owner decided to give up such luxuries as eating so that she could bring the colt to us to be straightened out.

We took the colt to the bronc pen and trained him to stand in hobbles and sideline. He snorted when the saddle and blanket were brought up, but there was little he could do about it. The semi-Quarter Horse saddle seemed to fit him fine. After we cinched the saddle down, we slipped a hackamore over his head. We removed the foot restraints and allowed him to wander around the pen. He didn't run or buck, so a rider mounted him. We went on in good shape, though he knew nothing. Later we drove him for a few minutes before a ride so he could learn to move out, turn, stop, and back up.

A new cheap saddle can be purchased wholesale for less than $400. I wanted more information about them, so I telephoned my wholesaler, who also happens to sell saddles. He carries top-of-the-line saddles but buys cheapies for resale. These saddles actually have wood trees covered with rawhide. The cheapest of cheapies have wood covered with canvas or fiber glass. The best of the cheap lot are covered with rawhide.

All of the cheap trees are "regular" width, that is, a gullet width of five and a half or five and three-fourths inches. With good trees the next size up is the semi-Quarter Horse, which has a six-inch gullet width. The Quarter Horse tree has a gullet of six and a half inches. The wide Quarter Horse has the six-and-a-half-inch gullet width with a wide flare to the bars.

The slope of the bars (the way the bars lie on a horse's back) is of great concern to saddlemakers and tree makers. The cheap trees are mass-produced with little attention given to fit. Such saddles have to be made of the cheapest material available and are put together with a staple gun rather than with good nails and screws. It's simply a matter of economics. The people who make cheapies have to economize to stay in business.

I too make saddles, so let's take a look at my material costs. My trees cost me at least $120. My last roll of leather cost more than $650 (ten sides), so each side costs $65. I

Not long ago it rained all day, so my riders cleaned tack. I asked them to experiment on rough-side-out leather, for we have several saddles with rough-out seats that are polished to a black mirror finish. It's nasty-looking and so slick it's like riding a greased hog. What we came up with really works.

We used Ivory soap, warm water, and a sponge to clean the saddles, and a *dull* butcher knife to scrape the seats. In a short time the rough seats were clean and again rough. This also works well to clean the old, dried sweat and horse dust from the inside of the fenders.

Saddle soap is designed to put the oils back into leather. You can't clean your hands with saddle soap, nor can you really clean leather with it. There are other soaps you can use, but I trust Ivory. Why? Because that's what we used in my youth for racetrack harness. Clean with Ivory, then use saddle soap.

Years ago most horses had saddle marks on each side of their withers. Breaking them with a saddle that didn't fit was the norm. Today you'll see few saddle marks on the better horses, which means that many riders are using saddles that fit their horses. We watch for dry spots (areas where the horse doesn't sweat) and realize that those are the tight places where the saddle rests, small places that take the pressure instead of its being distributed all over the back. Sometimes we see swelling in those areas after a long ride. If so, it's time to switch saddles on that horse.

If a colt when grown to a horse will wear a semi-Quarter Horse saddle, we start him in a Quarter Horse saddle. Over the years his back will shape a little to fit a saddle. He'll get a little thinner at the pressure points. This doesn't mean that we should use a narrow saddle on a wide horse.

I sincerely believe that you should take almost as much care selecting a saddle as you do when selecting a horse. See if you can try a saddle before buying it. This is fairly easy when buying a used, local saddle. It's nearly impossible when buying a new saddle, for, after you use it, it's no longer new.

Most of my saddle customers are a long distance away. We talk it all over on the telephone, however, and I usually get a pretty good idea of what they want.

The saddle should come down smoothly on both sides of the horse without resting on a couple of points. Use the blankets you normally use. Cinch up. Get on and test the gullet height. You should be able to get your fingers under the fork (the spot between the gullet and the horse's withers) easily. Check to see if you have plenty of clearance between the front of the seat and the withers. If it's a little wide, try it with a heavier blanket, or use a second blanket. Ride the horse for an hour to see if the saddle still fits well and that you aren't riding up on his neck or back over his rump. Many saddles "crawl" if your horse doesn't have a really good back.

Does the saddle seem stable, or could you pull it over to the side if you put your weight in a stirrup. If so, and if the saddle is cinched fairly tight, you have a dangerous situation.

Some horses have very prominent withers. A saddle isn't apt to turn on such a horse. A loose saddle, however, can work back and off the rear end. We have one such horse here now, and he must be equipped with a good breast collar.

At any rate, we know that we can't fit all horses with individual saddles. If you have one horse, try to fit him the best you can. If you have several, you have to fit the widest and pad the rest, or get several saddles.

# Index

## A

Accident prevention:161-70
Albion Laboratories: 226
Automatic waterers: 165

## B

Backing: 42, 84, 96, 131, 147, 148, 208-16
Backing collar: 148
Backup rope: 112, 121
Balkers: 193, 216, 229, 269-73
Barn sour: 227-32
"Bench knees": 6
Biting: 173-74
Bit guard: 46-47, 60-62, 66, 68, 254, 264
Bits: colt bit, 45, 60, 64, 230, 252; snaffle bit, 61-62, 127, 264-65;
    SM polo bit, 62-65; Pelham, 62, 64-66, 70, 109, 252, 266; spade,
    69-72; curb, 104, 254, 266; Salinas, 255-57; overbitting, 266
Blindfold: 24-25, 28, 98, 174, 201-202, 219-21, 273
Bone: 6
Boots: 77, 81, 84
Bosal: 107, 249-50
Breakaway hobbles: 205, 207
Breeding: 177-84
Breeding hobbles: 182-83
Bronc pen: 15-16, 20, 41-42, 165
Bucking: 15-16, 91, 187, 194, 263, 267-71, 277

## C

Canine teeth: 264
Cantering: 97
Catching Horses: 17-19, 28-32, 38, 164-65
Cinches: 262-63
Circling; 84-88, 93, 97, 230
Colic: 161-62, 165, 169-70
Collection: 95-96
Colt bit: *see* bits
Colts: early handling, 9-10; starting, 13-65; first rides, 48-53; early training, 48-65, 127; starting on cattle, 74, 81, 131-41; roping, 78-81; dry training, 83, 149-50
Conformation: 3-6, 103
Copper rollers: 64, 67
Cricket: 251, 257
Crop: 87, 264
Croup: 4-6
Cues: 52-55
Curb bit: *see* bits
Cutting costs: 157-60
Cutting horse: 48, 82, 126-27
Cutting horse training: 127-41
Cutting horse rules: 142-57
Cystic ovaries: 223-26

## D

Dally roping: 110, 112
Direct rein: 108, 245-46
Discipline: 183-86
Double reins: 108-109, 252
Doubling: 49-51, 74, 108, 131, 213, 246, 266
Draw reins: 46, 47, 61-62, 70, 253-54
Dwell: 53

## E

Ewe neck: 4, 100, 251

Eyes: 3, 216, 234-36, 240


F


Falling horses: 258-66
Feeding: 166
Fences: 162-64
Fiador: 45
Figure eight: 96-97
Flank cinch: 117
Flying changes: 97
Forefooting: 28, 275, 276
Forked trees: 164
Founder: 162, 165
Full pass: 94-96


G


Gaskin: 7
Gates: 164
Gear: 43-72
Ground driving: 24, 40-42


H


Hackamore: 43-44, 107, 213
Hackamore horse: 45, 60
Hackamore training: 48-60, 127, 130, 228-30, 246, 271
Half pass: 90, 94-95
Halter pullers: 20, 166-70
Hauling: 197, 200-202
Head set: 4
Head tossing: 28-29, 251, 253, 254
Heart girth: 4
Heat: 98
High-headed: 4, 72, 74, 117, 147-50, 251-54
Hip: 6
Hobbles and sideline: 19-20, 22-28, 98, 169, 174-77, 183, 218,

277-78
Hooves: 6-7, 33
Horses that bully: 267-69
Horse types: 103; hackamore horse, 45-60; snaffle-bit horse, 45-46
Hot walker: 190

## I

Insane horses: 250-51

## J

Jeffery method: 27-33, 36-39, 207, 223, 229, 275

## K

Kicking: 29, 217, 231, 275

## L

Lariats: 124-25
Leads: 59, 73, 88, 90-93; changes of lead, 96-97
Leg aids: 53-58, 83-84, 88, 91-92, 95, 104, 231
Leds: 6
Lightning: 163
Limber necking: 86-87
Loading: 197-98
Longeing: 10, 40

## M

Martingales: 46, 62, 70, 99, 109, 117, 251-54
Mecate: 43-45, 128-30
Mechanical hackamore: 43, 228, 266
Minerals: 224-26
Mona Lisa: 257

Mounting: 203-207, 263
"Mutton-withered": 4, 127
Muzzle: 3

# N

Neck: 4, 7-8
Neck rein: 85, 104, 107-108, 245

# P

Pelham bit: *see* bits
Pirouette: 103
Polo bit: *see* bits
Popper: 87, 238-40
Problems: 267-72
Punishment: 12

# Q

Quarters-in: 4-5, 92, 95

# R

Rearing: 193-94, 239-40, 245, 262-64, 266
Refusals: 195
Reined cow horse: 49, 77
Reining: 104-109, 147-49
Reining horse: 48, 82, 83
Reins: 107
Rewards: 12, 234, 250
Rollback: 53-55, 74-78, 132
Romal: 107
Roping: 17, 37-38, 42; calf roping, 78, 81; "Hoolihan," 80; rope
    horse, 82; rope horse training, 110-25; roper's box, 114-17
Runaways: 227
Running: 131, 227-32

## S

Sacking out: 273
Saddles: 90-91, 124, 189-90, 277-82; care, 4, 280-81
Saddle pads: 91, 117, 212, 231, 263
Saddling: 23, 24, 212, 248-49, 263, 277-78
Salinas bit: *see* bits
Scotch hobble: 26-27, 175, 183, 217-18, 274
Serpentine: 92
Shoulders: 4
Shoulders-in: 95-96
Slides: 82
Snaffle bit: *see* bits
Snubbing post: 20-21, 98, 169
Spade bit: *see* bits
Spins: 93, 99-104
Spooking and shying: 233-46
Spurs: 87-89, 138, 140, 212-13
Squaw rein: 104, 106, 107
Staking out: 168-69
Stallions, handling: 171-84
Stargazing: 70, 72, 261
Stifle: 7
Stops: 52-53, 55-58, 74-78, 82-84, 98, 117-18
"Straight up in the bridle": 71, 107-108
Striking: 218-19, 275
Sulkers: 216, 269, 273
Suppling: 86-88, 92
Surcingle: 86

## T

Tail wringing: 247-50
Team roping: 119, 122-24
Throwing: 26-28, 240, 245, 272-76
"Tied in at the knees": 6
Tie-downs: 117, 251, 261
Timid horses: 233-46
Toe in, toe out: 7
Tongue over bit: 264-65

Traps: 164-65
Turn-back rider:136
Twitch: 183, 219
Two-tracking: 4-5, 94-98
Tying front foot: 183, 274


U


Utah hobbles: 243


W


War bridle: 29, 223
Weight-shift cues: 51, 55-58, 84, 91-92, 104, 141
Whips: 198-99, 221, 223, 238-40, 264; misuse of, 18, 171-72, 181-82, 227, 234; dressage, 96-97, 148
Withers: 4, 127
Wolf teeth: 264
Worms: 161-62
Wright, Maurice ( *The Jeffery Method of Horse Handling* ): 28

*Practical Western Training,*

designed by Bill Cason, was set in various sizes of Garamond by the University of Oklahoma Press and printed offset on 60-pound Glatfelter B-31 by Cushing Malloy, Inc., with case binding by John H. Dekker & Sons.